Young Writers

2004 POETRY COMPETITION

GW00691692

ONC
A R

IMAGINATION FOR
A NEW GENERATION

Belfast

Edited by Steve Twelvetree

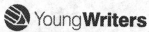 Young**Writers**

First published in Great Britain in 2004 by:
Young Writers
Remus House
Coltsfoot Drive
Peterborough
PE2 9JX
Telephone: 01733 890066
Website: www.youngwriters.co.uk

SB ISBN 1 84460 448 9

Foreword

Young Writers was established in 1991 and has been passionately devoted to the promotion of reading and writing in children and young adults ever since. The quest continues today. Young Writers remains as committed to engendering the fostering of burgeoning poetic and literary talent as ever.

This year's Young Writers competition has proven as vibrant and dynamic as ever and we are delighted to present a showcase of the best poetry from across the UK. Each poem has been carefully selected from a wealth of *Once Upon A Rhyme* entries before ultimately being published in this, our twelfth primary school poetry series.

Once again, we have been supremely impressed by the overall high quality of the entries we have received. The imagination, energy and creativity which has gone into each young writer's entry made choosing the best poems a challenging and often difficult but ultimately hugely rewarding task - the general high standard of the work submitted amply vindicating this opportunity to bring their poetry to a larger appreciative audience.

We sincerely hope you are pleased with our final selection and that you will enjoy *Once Upon A Rhyme Belfast* for many years to come.

Contents

Rachel Drain (11)	17
Nathan Wilson (8)	17
Kelly Sloan (8)	18
Emma Graham (9)	18
Ryan McCullough (9)	19
Daniel Rea (9)	19
Hayley Anderson (8)	20
Luke Frizzell (9)	20
Jessica Mooney (8)	21
Eimear Lambe (9)	21
Philip Kelly (9)	22
Naomi Sharratt (9)	22
Caelán Trodden (9)	22
Michael Devlin (9)	23
Conal Begley (9)	23
Rebecca Gonsalves (10)	23
Amy Crawford (9)	24
Niamh Macpherson (8)	24
Stacey Wilkinson (9)	25
Duncan MacMillan (8)	25
Simon Watters (8)	26

Euston Street Primary School

Jemma Gibson (8)	26
Robyn Todd (8)	26
Eryn Duff (11)	27
Deborah Murphy (7)	27
Robert Irvine (7)	27
Gareth Yates (8)	28
Jenna Parker (7)	28

Finaghy Primary School

Amy McCrea (11)	28
Hayley Brush (8)	29
Chei-Tim Chung (10)	30
Jordan Bradley (9)	31
Amy Robb (11)	31
Corey Colin Johnston (9)	32
Haydn McKenna (11)	32
Glenn Stephens (11)	33
Nichola Luney (11)	33

Gaelscoil Na Bhfál

David Nelson (10)   51
Turlough Lavery (8)   52
Liam McMahon (10)   54
Aoibh McLaughlin (8)   54
Emma McDonald (10)   55
Lee McCann (9)   55
Fionnghuala Higgins (9)   56
Patrice Kelly (10)   56
Megan Weir (9)   57
Clíodhna Morrison (11)   58
Pádraig McBride (10)   58
Paul Nolan (11)   59
Sinead Campbell (11)   59
Niamh Burns (11)   60
Jim O'Hanlon (10)   61

Holy Rosary Primary School

Elizabeth Murphy (10)   61
Sarah McGrenaghan (11)   62
Emma Moreland (10)   62
Paul Stelges (11)   63
Conall Bailie (11)   63
Lauren Little (11)   63
Louise McLaughlin (11)   64
Laura Curry (10)   65
Paul Maguire Wilson (10)   65
Glenn King (11)   65
Conor Stewart (11)   66
Anna Carr (11)   66
Bebhinn Schaible (10)   67
Daniel Robinson (10)   67

Knockbreda Primary School

Rebecca McKee (10)   67
Kyle Dugan (9)   68
Philip Davison (9)   68
James Connery (10)   69
Niamh Weir (9)   69
Luke McCann (9)   70
Victoria Carson (8) & Christine Collins (9)   70
Stuart Lammey (10)   71

John Lynn (10)   71
Matthew Deane (9)   72

Malvern Primary School

Jonathan Goddard (10)	72
Courtney Cinnamon (8)	72
Shannon Brownlee (9)	73
Ashleigh Gaynor (9)	73
Cody McMillan (8)	73
Philip Morrison (9)	74
Craig Harrison (9)	74
Nicole McDowell (8)	74
Megan Hollyoak (9)	75
William Morton (9)	75
Kyle Morton (9)	75
Natasha Haveron (7)	76
Jonathan McCallion (8)	76
Aaron Patterson (8)	76
Jordan McAuley (8)	76
Curtis Griffiths (8)	77
Jemma McKittrick (7)	77
Daniel Fisher (7)	77
Connor Irvine (8)	77

Mersey Street Primary School

Sarah Wilkinson (8)	78
Taylor Gray (8)	78
Edmund Green (11)	79
Samuel Conlane (10)	79
Adam Swain (9)	79
Dean Proctor (10)	80
Nicole Palmer (10)	80
Ryan Giltrap (9)	80
Sarah-Louise Laverty (9)	81
Martin Kemp (10)	81
Alan Fisher (9)	81
Luke Wilson (9)	82
Curtis Wynne (10)	82
Aaron Clarke (10)	82

St Bernadette's Primary School, Ballymurphy

Melissa Seawright (8)	83
Sara Louise Murphy (9)	83
Kerry Stone (8)	84
Danielle McKnight (9)	84
Megan O'Hare (9)	85
Jamie Wallace (9)	85
Lauren Clarke (9)	86
Danielle O'Donoghue (8)	86
Kerry-Ann Rainey (9)	87
Kirsty Hughes (9)	87
Samantha Morgan (9)	88
Lauren Hyland (9)	88

St Catherine's Primary School, Belfast

Seaneen O'Hara (11)	89
Courtney Di Lucia (10)	89
Rachael McLean (10)	90
Elisha Black (10)	90
Zoe Burns (10)	91
Rebecca Ainsworth (10)	91
Rebecca McCormick (8)	92
Bronagh O'Prey (10)	92
Megan McBride (9)	93
Stephanie McKeown (11)	93
Maureen Turner (10)	94
Jolene Ann McFarlane (10)	94
Laurie-Ann Mary Bartsch (9)	95
Megan Rose (9)	95
Michaela Mulholland (9)	96
Sammy-Jo Madden (10)	96
Rachel Annesley (9)	97
Patricia Savage (9)	97
Sarah Graham (9)	98
Eileen Donnelly (8)	98
Margaret-Rose Tully (10)	99
Kelly-Anne McCullough (10)	99
Gemma Kearney (9)	99
Mary-Louise Bunting (10)	100
Siobhan Cunningham (10)	100
Kirsten Brannigan (10)	100

Nicola Moyes (11)   101
Niamh Flynn (9)   101
Hannah Murray (10)   101
Stacey Quinn (10)   102
Emma Magee (8)   102

St Gall's Primary School, Belfast

Pearse Conor Mooney (8)   103
Patrick Kilifin (8)   103
Donn Whelan (8)   104
Gary Marron (8)   104
Matthew Walker (8)   104
Nathan Maginn (7)   105
Daniel Donnan (8)   105
Ryan Casson (8)   106
James Brennan (8)   106
Michael Meehan (7)   107
Niall Carson (8)   107
Ciaran Donnelly (9)   107
Conor Malone (8)   108
Fiontain Kennedy (9)   108
Stephen Maginn (9)   109
Aaron Slane (7)   109

St John The Baptist Boys' Primary School, Belfast

Eamonn Quinn (10)   110
Colm Molloy (11)   110
Ryan Bowman (11)   110
Conor Donnelly (9)   111
Michael Duffin (9)   111
Conor McGrath (9)   112
Conal Sheppard (9)   112
Ryan Hegarty (9)   113
Louis Donnelly (9)   113
Gareth May (10)   114
Gary Crossan (10)   115
Jonathan Morrissey (11)   116
Gerard O'Rawe (10)   116
Peter Forde (11)   117
Kurtis McGreevy (11)   117
Michael Adair (11)   117

Eoghan Murray (10) 118
Emmet McPoland (11) 118
Karl Dowdall (10) 119
Darren Cosgrove (11) 119
Damien Barton (9) 119

St Mark's Primary School, Dunmurry

Alanna Flynn (8) 120
Caitlin Duffy (8) 120
Gary Campbell Smyth (9) 120
Nadeen Whelan (8) 120
Thomas Hughes (9) 121
Anthony Rooney (9) 121
Dominic O'Prey (9) 121
Thomas Kerr (8) 121
Joshua Galway (11) 122
Claire Begley (9) 122
Kelly Duffy (11) 123
Hannah Denvir (9) 123
Nathan McGonnell (9) 124
Eoin Curley (9) 124
Christina Magennis (9) 124
Shauna Briggs (10) 125
Georgia Perry (9) 125
Andrew Kettle (8) 125
Courtney Thomas (8) 126
Niamh Hamill (9) 126
Gabriella Norney (9) 127
Leia Corr (9) 127
Conor Moylan (8) 127
Tanya McCarry (10) 127
James McDermott (9) 128
Mark Ormerod (10) 128
Thomas Manning (10) 129
Lauren McMahon (10) 129
Gerard McAreavey (10) 129
Djamila Boudissa (11) 130
Mark Walsh (11) 130
Ashton McLaughlin (10) 130
Noel Bradley-Johnston (10) 131
Louise McClenaghan (11) 131

Corey Hamill (10)	132
Emma Brown (11)	132
Patrick Hope (11)	132
Michael McConnell (10)	133
Zachary Gordon (10)	133
Gavin McKee (11)	133
James Maguire (9)	134
Devina Whelan (11)	134
Brendan McStravick (10)	134
Michelle Russell (9)	135
Kirsty Mulligan (9)	135
Christopher Keenan (9)	136
Natasha McCann (10)	136
Stephanie Brown (10)	137
Ashleigh McManus (10)	137
Matthew Cassidy (8)	137
Niamh Kelly (9)	138
Mary Rose Duffy (9)	138
Rebecca May (10)	139
Ruairi Carlile (8)	139
James McShane (10)	140
Shannon McKee (9)	140
Sinead McParland (10)	141
Karen McClenaghan (9)	141
Deborah Kennedy (10)	141
Mark Mahon (11)	142
Orlaith Molloy (11)	143
Anthony Speers (11)	144
Timothy Bradley (11)	145
Anthony Todd (11)	146
Tommy Davidson (11)	147
Daniel Maloney (11)	148
Lisa McMahon (11)	149
Michael Lyons (11)	150
James Todd (11)	151
Jennifer Kerr (11)	152
Gerard McKeown (11)	153
Bronagh McKenna (11)	154
Laura Allen (11)	155
Ciara Moylan (10)	156
Kevin Quinn (10)	156
Kelly McCleave (11)	157

Siobhán McCullough (9)   158
Angela Diamond (10)   158
Lisa McAreavey (9)   159
Taylor Murtagh (8)   159
Jackie Johnson (9)   160
Samantha Murphy (10)   160
Ryan Magee (9)   160
Shauna Hamill (10)   161
Marcus Owens (10)   161
Daragh McGuinness (10)   161
Christopher Herald (9)   162
Aidan Devlin (9)   162
Niamh Walker (10)   163
Matthew O'Donnell (10)   163
James Norney (10)   164
Naomi Smith (9)   164
Maria Adams (10)   164
Dean McDonagh (11)   165
Rachel Whelan (11)   166
Caoimhe McDonald (11)   167
Amanda O'Prey (11)   168
Jonathan Donnelly (11)   169
Samantha Gourley (10)   169

St Michael's Primary School, Belfast

Andrew Gunn (10)   170
Matthew McCormick (11)   170
Laura Vinelott (11)   171
Alice Donaldson (11)   171
Odhran McIntaggart (11)   171
Eithne Fraser (11)   172
Timothy Durkan (10)   172
James Day (11)   173
Emma Nicholson (10)   173
Leenane Mellotte (10)   173
Siofra Berndt (10)   174
Ryan McGuckin (11)   174
Isobel Clarke (10)   175
Declan King (11)   175
Erin Sykes (11)   176
Roisin McAlister (11)   176

The Poems

My Sister Ella

My sister Ella is so funny
She hops around like a bunny
She likes to play with money
When she gets a meal
She throws it on the floor
Then she does it even more
She crawls
And she sometimes falls
She walks
And talks
She likes cartoons
She's mad as baboons
She sometimes likes balloons
But she bursts them
When she watches cartoons
She turns them off
She sometimes pretends to cough
She climbs onto the sofa
She likes wearing skirts
She pulls the cushion off the sofa
She jumps all over me
And that's the way my sister Ella is.

Kyle Sherman (10)
Beechfield Primary School

Dancing Poem

I dance to that beat
And kick my feet
I move to the rhythm
Of the sound in my street

I love to dance
I love to sing
I love to move
With that music thing!

Shannon Millen (10)
Beechfield Primary School

Guess Who?

I have a waggly tail,
I chew on mail.
I have four little paws
And very sharp claws.

I have fluffy fur
And I am as cuddly as a bear.
I have floppy ears
And cry puppy tears.

I'm a bone eater
And a good sleeper,
I'm a kiss giver
And I'm cute forever.

Have you guessed who I am?

I'm a puppy!

Chevelle Shields (11)
Beechfield Primary School

Guess Who!

I shine a lot,
As bright as the sun!
I like to shoot
And have lots of fun!

Astronomers like me,
Yes! It's true!
I've told you a lot now,
Can you guess who?

My mother is the moon,
I'm the brightest by far!
In the night we spread,
Yes! I'm a star!

Rebecca Wilson (10)
Beechfield Primary School

Snow

The snow is
As cold as milk
Soft and watery
Cold as ice.

The snow is
As shiny as a diamond
Hard and smooth
Like a star.

The snow is
Like a polar bear
Soft and warm
Like a blanket.

The snow is
Like a wedding dress
Sparkly and long
Like frost.

Orrianne Farr (8)
Beechfield Primary School

The Moon

The moon
Is round
Like a ball

The moon
Is round
As a clock

The moon
Is round
Like a hole.

Daniel Messruther (8)
Beechfield Primary School

The Moon

The moon is like
snow when it falls
from the sky, it is cold as ice.

The moon is like
an eyeball when you
move your eye.

The moon is like
a ball, it is white
and it is bouncy.

The moon is like
the sun shining in
the sky and the sun is hot.

Lauren Hunter (9)
Beechfield Primary School

Cars

Some cars are fast
Some cars are slow
But no matter what
They take you where
You want to go.

Some cars are red
Some cars are blue
But no matter what
It's what suits you.

Tammy Upton (11)
Beechfield Primary School

My Brother Aaron

My brother Aaron
Wants to be a footballer,
Last year he wanted to be a DJ.
He can't make up his mind,
He's useless with choices all day long,
He needs to work hard at school
To be a footballer.
His fave music is rave music,
His fave football teams are
Liverpool, Rangers and Glentorn.
He really wants to be a footballer all day long.

Nicola Stewart (9)
Beechfield Primary School

My Brother Daniel

My brother Daniel
Has a favourite football team:
Rangers
Daniel copied Jeff
At first
He thought it was good, he still does.
My brother wants
To be in the army
When he grows up.

Naomi Whyte (9)
Beechfield Primary School

The Moon

The moon is
As dark as blood
Flowing.

The moon is
As round as the world
Turning around.

The moon is
Like a cat's face
Looking at me.

The moon looks
As white as snow
Falling.

The moon looks
Like a football
Flying in the air.

Steven Storey (9)
Beechfield Primary School

The Frosty Day

The frost is like
A freezer and keeps
Things cold.

The frost is like
A block of ice
And it's cold.

The frost is slippery
As banana skins
Make you fall.

Frost is like snow
Which makes you fall
And skid.

Laura Davison (9)
Beechfield Primary School

Winter

Winter
Doffs his hat to let the wind blow
His mouth opens, snowstorms roll in
His eyes blink evilly
He waves his ragged coat
His slim and bony fingers turn you to ice.
He wears black ripped trousers
And long leather boots
His long spindly arms and legs
Make the icy ground crack.
When the moon is very high
When the sun is very low
Winter's big tall body is always on the go
Hailstones fall from his big long nose
His dark eyes are cunning and wild
Dropping spells of rain.

Hannah Breen (10)
Cairnshill Primary School

Winter

Jack Frost
Blinks icy snowflakes
His silvery eyes weep blizzards
His pointed nose drips hailstones
His jagged mouth spits out lightning
His dead arms wave, snow blankets the landscape
His bony fingers touch you, your cheeks turn numb
His crippled feet run, ice coats the world
His top hat blows off, avalanches tumble
His ripped cloak sweeps out, covering the world
His patched trousers drizzle snowflakes at you
His suede boots launch snowstorms.

Lee Carser (10)
Cairnshill Primary School

Winter

Winter's
Icy fingers touch your
Cheek
You're chilled to the bone
His mouth
Opens
Hear the winds moan
He takes off
His hat
Icy rivers flow
He swirls
His cloak
And savage gales blow
He waves
Thin arms
And it begins to snow
He sneers
With jagged teeth
And the sun is set low
He runs
And the world is covered in frost
When he makes
It snow
All grass is lost
He remembers spring
Will be here in one day
And sneers
I must make a
Quick getaway!

Ben McCullough (10)
Cairnshill Primary School

Winter

Winter's
Icy fingers touch your cheek
And you are left in his icy prison,
Where escape is impossible to seek
His eyes blink crystalline tears,
Which freeze the paths
And as he dances through the snow,
He cruelly laughs:
All the little children asleep in their beds
Will soon have chilly toes and noses that are red!

His old bowler hat that has been moth-eaten
And his tatty old coat that is badly wind beaten,
Will be no more,
Once spring has knocked on his door.

Katie Millar (10)
Cairnshill Primary School

One Hallowe'en A Firework Went Off

One Hallowe'en
A firework went off
I covered my ears
But all I saw
Was the light
Going off
I let go of my ears
Because I thought that
It was all over
But suddenly
A big
Boom went off.
Then my mum
Told me that
Light goes faster
Than sound.

David Meehan (8)
Cranmore Integrated Primary School

The Sounds Of Night-Time

The sounds in the night-time
Go all through our house,
The tick-tock of our clock
And the sound of the tiny mouse,
The footsteps of children
Upon the top floor.

The crick in the floorboards
And the creak of the chairs,
The sound of the doorbell
Is the arrival of guests,
The clashes of dishes
As dinner commences,
Then the babble of voices
That distance makes thin.

Joanna Lavery (11)
Cranmore Integrated Primary School

Autumn Poem

In the autumn I see falling leaves
Turning amber, red and brown
Hedgehogs are hibernating for the winter
Stars are shining bright at night

I go to bed and hear the leaves rustling
The fireworks bang, whee, fizz
The wind howls and it's getting cold
And I hear ghostly noises outside my window

When I go outside I smell the fresh leaves
I smell the smoke from the bonfires
I smell the earthy smell from my garden
I can't see because of the misty air.

Hollie Thomson (9)
Cranmore Integrated Primary School

Birds In My Garden

B irds are chirping in the trees on a sunny morning.
I am woken up by their song like a dream, I sleep on.
R acket to some the birds might be, but just watch them as
D iving through the air they come to feed on the plum
S plattered on the ground.

O bese, colourful, happy, hopping on the mound
N ever seen out when a cat is around.

A back door bangs!

S cared they flee to the hedge out of sight, shivering, petrified,
U nscathed they are waiting, watching -
N othing!
N ot a cat, not a human in sight
Y et unknown and unexpected the cat creeps up on the birds.

M ercilessly the cat lies waiting.
O ne bird at a time returns to the feeders
R ight where the cat lies.
N ow is its chance!
I t climbs the tree at top speed -
N othing?
G one!

Connor Montgomery (10)
Cranmore Integrated Primary School

Inside My Head

A match between Kyle and Matthew
And we needed football shoes
But Matthew had none
And there were no nets
Then we found some and I won
We made another match
But this time Matthew won.

Kyle McLaughlin (9)
Cranmore Integrated Primary School

Week Of Winter Weather

On Monday hailstones missiled down
and tried to crack my crown,

Tuesday's sky was clear and dry
as we walked it started to cry,

On Wednesday burst of rain
filled up the drain,

Thursday stood out foggy and mild,
if you don't believe me ask any child,

Friday's frost was horribly cold,
enough to grow an icy mould,

Saturday's sky black, cloudy and dark
I couldn't get out to lark,

Sunday was Christmas Eve and snow was falling
I was filled with glee.

Katie Keenan-Fulton (10)
Cranmore Integrated Primary School

Similes To Describe Winter

A winter's morning is like
Showering like falling hailstones,
Freezing like sharp needles injected into your body,
White as a white city,
Dark as a blackout.

A winter's morning is like
Frost and a blizzard,
Windy like a gust of wind,
Snowing like a storm,
Frozen like time stopped.

Jamie Kennedy (10)
Cranmore Integrated Primary School

If . . .

If I were an animal I would be a cheetah
So I could run over hills and mountains
I would run very fast
And chase other animals.

If I were a colour I would be yellow
Like a bright flower
And be bright like the sun shining down on the water.

Charlotte Millen (10)
Cranmore Integrated Primary School

Inside My Head

A bird made from books
A room full of toys
A new car for Christmas
A holiday for my birthday
To learn all of my tables
To do well in my art club
To get to school early every morning
To have an nice lunch every day.

Ash Power (10)
Cranmore Integrated Primary School

Rain

Rain is like the sun crying tears
Saying, 'Why can't I come out to play today?'
Rain is like a waterfall,
Crashing,
Sprinkling,
Leaping
Softly falling to the pool below.

Victoria Reilly (10)
Cranmore Integrated Primary School

Rain

Rain is like falling cats and dogs
Crashing down on the ground
Rain is like dancing feet
Running down the drain
Rain is like a waterfall
Splashing
    Falling
        Crashing
            Dripping
                Falling into a big hole.

Hannah Massey-Dickson (10)
Cranmore Integrated Primary School

If

If I were an animal
I would be a cheetah
So that I could run at other animals
Jump up and down.

If I were a colour
I would be brown
Like leaves
And fall off the trees
Running along the ground.

Matthew Herd (9)
Cranmore Integrated Primary School

Acrostic Name Poem

D angerous Drew who
R uns as fast as he can
E ducationally intelligent
W ith lots of friends.

Drew Maxwell (9)
Cranmore Integrated Primary School

Seasons Of The World

Spring arrived through winter snow,
The cold clutch has let me go,
The sun is here,
The first season has decided to appear.

Summer hit with a blast,
But the sun is not to last,
The trees will soon not be here,
The second season has appeared.

Autumn's here, trees are bare,
The summer's beauty is in despair,
Summer's left, it's not here,
The third season has got to appear.

Winter storm has finally hit,
Knocked the leaves to their pit,
Warmth and sun have left here,
The fourth season ain't that bad - Christmas is near!

Jamie Doyle (10)
Cranmore Integrated Primary School

Week Of Winter Weather

On Monday bitter winds blow around
the streets making people not want to go out.

Tuesday's hailstones are crashing
and bashing people with stone.

Wednesday's snow comes down
as rain turns into ice.

Thursday stood out nice with breeze.

Friday, well that was the life.

Aaron Brady (10)
Cranmore Integrated Primary School

Autumn

Leaves are falling round my body,
Fluttering at my feet,
Squirrels collecting nuts,
Smell the fresh wind mmm . . .

Night sky lights up with fireworks,
Turning colour gold, bronze, red, amber
As I walk through the forest
I hear leaves crunching

The fireworks going different colours
Boom, bang, pop!
Their colours are red, blue, purple,
Witches, pumpkins, ghosts

Coming to get you . . . boo!

Emma Jane Mackenzie (9)
Cranmore Integrated Primary School

Football Poem

When I was very small
My favourite toy was the big football
I played with you from dawn to dusk
Still chewing my baby rusk

As I get older you are still
My favourite form of pep-up pill
I jump out of bed and check to see
If you are there to play with me

You and I are the best of friends
I hope our friendship never ends
Football, football I love you
Football, football you're so cool!

Aimée McKeown (10)
Cranmore Integrated Primary School

I Wish, I Wish

I wish, I wish upon a star
That the world will turn into a candy bar
That the trees will turn to lollipops
And that farmers won't grow such yucky crops

I wish, I wish upon a pond
That I shall be so very fond
Of the chocolate lake around my back
And the fruit and vegetables will start to lack

I wish, I wish upon all glory
That I shall drive a chewing gum lorry
I shall blow a gigantic bubble
I wonder if I'll get in trouble?

But still I want a marshmallow bed
And a cream puff pillow to rest my head
But wait, there's more I can recall
A lickable wallpaper upon my wall

But then again how very sad
When I think of the healthy food I've had
But I know what's good for me
I'll have baked beans for my tea
We all know that they're good for your heart
But unfortunately they make you f***!

Rachel Drain (11)
Cranmore Integrated Primary School

Lightning

Lightning can be bright,
It's white like a light
Shining all across the sea like a light.
It's scary and frightening,
Nobody knows when it's going to strike.

Nathan Wilson (8)
Cranmore Integrated Primary School

Thunder And Lightning

Thunder and lightning
Sounds quite frightening
Knocking trees all about
I started to scream
Then my mum gave a shout
'I'm trying to sleep can't you see
You're a chatterbox
You drink too much tea!'
Then I got so angry
I started to weep
'Sssshhh! I'm trying to sleep!'
'It is not me
It's the thunder and lightning
Can't you see
You always blame it on me!'

Kelly Sloan (8)
Cranmore Integrated Primary School

A Windy Day And Rain

Clothes swishing around,
Blowing in the air,
Dresses going everywhere.
Socks spinning around,
Flying in the air.
Swishing forwards, backwards
Any single way.
Rain lashing down
Run outside grab the clothes
Run back inside
Stick the clothes in the dryer.
Wait a minute then
They will be as dry
And clean as can be.

Emma Graham (9)
Cranmore Integrated Primary School

The Flying Boy

I woke up one morning
All of a sudden I heard a roar
It was a windy day
As I ran out the door
And I heard a voice
It was the wind
It said, 'Fly Ryan fly'
And it lifted me up
Like a spirit in the sky
I flew some distance
And then it calmed down
I said, 'Oh dear, not good'
Just before I hit the ground
I was floating again
As light as a feather
After that I am not going
Out again in windy weather.

Ryan McCullough (9)
Cranmore Integrated Primary School

Playing With Snow

Snow is soft and with it
You can do so much.
Playing with snow,
By making balls and throwing them
At family or friends.
You can make a snowman
And snow angels,
But you can't bring them in at night.

Daniel Rea (9)
Cranmore Integrated Primary School

Dancing Snowflakes

A snowflakes drops,
Sparkling in the air
It twists and turns
And lands on the ground
Like a white rug all around.
Dancing snowflakes
Dancing snowflakes.

As I look up in the sky
Cold white flakes
In my eyes
It sparkles, it sparkles
Like diamonds on the ground.

Dancing snowflakes
Dancing snowflakes.

Hayley Anderson (8)
Cranmore Integrated Primary School

The Snow

The snow is as cold as ice
But it is very nice
It can make my garden white as flour
It only takes half an hour
Kids playing snowball fights
Building snowmen too
Everywhere I go there is snow
It sticks to me like glue.

Luke Frizzell (9)
Cranmore Integrated Primary School

Thunder And Lightning

Sometimes I look outside
At the thunder and lightning
On a cold, dark, rainy night.
I often wonder, *what is thunder?*
It rumbles through the sky
After a blast of lightning
Hits and makes me wonder, *why . . . why*
Does it make this sound?
It sounds like the heavens above
Are applauding the performance
Of the lightning but . . .
What is this
Lightning?
But . . . what is this
Lightning?
It is like bright
Sparkles in the sky.

Jessica Mooney (8)
Cranmore Integrated Primary School

Snow

Snow, snow where do you go,
When the sun comes out to play?
Snow, snow we miss you so,
In the light of the day
In a very odd way
All the pears and fruits are now gone
The trees are bare
And the streets are white
And they look very soft
In all your months of winter.

Eimear Lambe (9)
Cranmore Integrated Primary School

Thunder And Lightning

Thunder and lightning are such a good team
If there was none it wouldn't be fun,
Just one night I heard a noise
I thought I was having a dream
I woke up, it was not a dream,
I heard it get closer,
It was the sound of thunder,
Then I saw fast yellow streaks.
Then I noticed it was thunder and lightning
So I watched it for a while
And then it faded away and disappeared.

Philip Kelly (9)
Cranmore Integrated Primary School

I Am The Sun

I am a ball of bright fire,
I light up the Earth,
I give warmth to the world,
I rise up at dawn like a giant orange,
I shine in the sky every day
Who am I?
I am the sun.

Naomi Sharratt (9)
Cranmore Integrated Primary School

Snow

I love the cold
It is like lying on an ice cube
I fall from the sky
I cover everything in my path
Like a white rug everything
Is white as a cloud on a sunny day.

Caelán Trodden (9)
Cranmore Integrated Primary School

Inside My Head

A Scalectrix for Christmas
A rocket for Hallowe'en
A room full of books
A rocket flying through space
A bird made from shoes
A petrol scooter for Christmas
A room full of sweets.

Michael Devlin (9)
Cranmore Integrated Primary School

Thunder And Lightning

Like fireworks in the sky
Very noisy not polite
Get zapped and your hair spikes up
Like giant thorns
Crash and *bang!* The sound of thunder
Lightning lights the sky up yonder
People scream running in through their gate
As for me, I think it's great.

Conal Begley (9)
Cranmore Integrated Primary School

Harvest

Sweet small sweetcorn
Precious prickly pineapple
Rising rough rice
Crunchy crumble coconut
Bunchy bursting bananas
Crunchy crispy carrots
We will eat all for tea
Come to our harvest and join in with me.

Rebecca Gonsalves (10)
Cranmore Integrated Primary School

Mr Rain

Pitter-patter
Pitter-patter
On my windowpane
Pitter-patter
Pitter-patter
Is it Mr Rain?
It's running fast
It shouldn't last
Pitter-patter
Pitter-patter
Is driving me insane!

Amy Crawford (9)
Cranmore Integrated Primary School

The Storm

Like fireworks flashing in the sky,
A loud rumble of thunder passes by.
The wind whizzes past so very fast,
I catch my breath, how long will it last?
I run indoors and watch the rain,
Beating against my windowpane.
The lightning flashes up on high,
Bright yellow in the midnight sky.
The wind has made my cheeks all rosy,
I go to bed and feel all cosy.
I'll stay there till the storm goes away,
I hope tomorrow will be a better day.

Niamh Macpherson (8)
Cranmore Integrated Primary School

The Wet Morning

The
        ground
                is
                        wet

My
        hair
                is
                        soaked

There
        are
                puddles
                        everywhere

My
        coat
                is
                        soaking

It
        is
                very
                        dark.

Stacey Wilkinson (9)
Cranmore Integrated Primary School

Storms

W hizzing past trees
E lectrocuting people
A killing storm
T earing through villages
H ating everything
E ating towns and cities
R aging through countries.

Duncan MacMillan (8)
Cranmore Integrated Primary School

The Feelings Of Weather

The sun only comes out when I'm happy
And the rain comes out when I'm sad,
But then I just think what it would be like to feel nothing at all
My heart would have to feel small
And now I can't care if I'm happy or sad,
But I will always always be glad
When I'm angry the thunder comes out
And the lightning roars,
When it's snowing I'm feeling okay
Just ready to play.

Simon Watters (8)
Cranmore Integrated Primary School

My Favourite Toys

I have a little bunny
That really is quite funny.
I will wear my groovy shades
When I'm on my Rollerblades.
I love my little scooter.
It has a shiny hooter.
But my favourite toy of all
Is Clair. She's my baby doll.

Jemma Gibson (8)
Euston Street Primary School

Little Robin Redbreast

One day I met a robin,
He was friendly as can be.
He knew that I would feed him,
If he would stay close to me.
Through summer and winter long,
Robin sang a cheery song.

Robyn Todd (8)
Euston Street Primary School

The Seven Seas

Roam the seven seas
Searching for jewels and diamonds
Roam the seven seas
Searching for souls and islands
Roam the seven seas
Listening or the waves that soar
Roam the seven seas
Listening for the mermaids' roar
Roam the seven seas.

Eryn Duff (11)
Euston Street Primary School

Kitten/Cat

Kitten, kitten, kitten,
As you run around
Kitten, kitten, kitten,
Please stay on the ground.

Kitten, kitten, kitten,
As you run and flee,
Kitten, kitten, kitten,
You mean so much to me.

Deborah Murphy (7)
Euston Street Primary School

Susie

I have a dog called Susie.
Her colours are black and white.
When I take her out a walk
She ends up in a fight.

Robert Irvine (7)
Euston Street Primary School

The Day I Was Born

The day I was born I couldn't open my eyes.
The day I was born I was fast asleep.
The day I was born I couldn't see a thing.
The day I was born I couldn't stand up.
The day I was born there was nothing to eat.
The day I was born I didn't want to go home.

Gareth Yates (8)
Euston Street Primary School

The Cat

The black and white cat,
who lived with young Pat,
fell asleep on the mat,
because he was tired
from chasing the rat.

Jenna Parker (7)
Euston Street Primary School

Sounds Down On The Shore

The seagulls squeal
The children cheer
The wind whistles
Down on the shore

The sea splashes
The crabs clap
The whales wail
Down on the shore

The puppies pant
The wet sand squelches
The boats bash
Down on the shore.

Amy McCrea (11)
Finaghy Primary School

Seasons

Spring is when the lambs are born,
You'll see them leaping in the morn.
The daffodils are blooming
And April showers are looming.
The blossom starts to bud,
While squirrels scamper through the mud.

Summer is when the sun shines bright
And sunglasses shade us from the light.
Now that we have finished school,
We can play in our paddling pool.
Whenever my friends and I went out,
All we did was scream and shout.

Autumn is when the nights are dark
And it's too wet and blustery to go to the park.
The leaves on the ground go snap, crackle, crunch,
So I pick them up in a great big bunch.
With their beautiful orange, brown and red,
I throw them high up over my head.

Winter is when the snow falls down
And covers the rooftops all over town.
We make lots of snowballs and have a big fight,
Then warm by the fire when we finish at night.
Santa comes to leave lots of toys,
But only for good little girls and boys.

Now I've described all the seasons
And given a few of my favourite reasons.
I like all the seasons in different ways,
But summer's my favourite with long sunny days.

Do you have a favourite and can you say why?
Think of a reason - go on give it a try!

Hayley Brush (8)
Finaghy Primary School

Seasons

The winter has gone,
The spring has come,
Happy are some.
The flowers are budding,
See the bird singing.
The sun has come to stay,
This money cannot pay.
It feels like summer is coming,
But it is only the beginning.

The sun shines all day and night,
In its glory and light.
Lots of children you'll see,
Splashing in the sea.
The sun is setting down,
See the beautiful sunset in town.
It's getting a bit colder
And I'm nearly one year older.

The trees are changing clothes,
As the wind blows.
The leaves are falling every day,
On the ground the fallen leaves lay.
Rain everywhere
Out of the window, there I stare.

Snow falls on the ground,
Children play every day.
Snowmen tall and white.

Chei-Tim Chung (10)
Finaghy Primary School

I Like Being Me

My mum is a cook,
My dad cements walls,
My brother is a pain in the bum,
But I'm nothing at all.

I can't knit,
I can't write a book,
I can't sing,
I can't even cook.

I'd try to swim,
But I'd only sink,
A lifeboat would come and save me,
Before I could think.

I wasn't much help,
When a cat got stuck in a tree
The only thing I'm good at
Is just being *me!*

Jordan Bradley (9)
Finaghy Primary School

A Passion For Fashion

Shoppin', shoppin', I love shoppin'
Shoppin', shoppin', with my eyes a poppin'
Runnin' in, runnin' out
Come on and glam about

Grabbin' this, grabbin' that
Hi mirror! I'm not fat
Tryin' on lots of clothes
Shoppin', shoppin', now strike a pose.

Amy Robb (11)
Finaghy Primary School

If I Were A Knight

If I were a knight
They would call me Sir Glory
The tales of my sights
Would tell a great story

I would protect the young
If they were in need
I would use my shield
And my sword indeed

I would guard the princess
Up in a high tower
To defeat a huge dragon
Would take lots of power

The king would give me a medal
For being strong and clever
And people would remember me
Forever and ever

At the end of the day
When I take my rest
I would say a long prayer
And hope for the best.

Corey Colin Johnston (9)
Finaghy Primary School

Fred

There once was a man called Fred
Who wasn't quite right in the head
He liked to smoke
While drinking his Coke
And now old Fred is dead.

Haydn McKenna (11)
Finaghy Primary School

Why Do My Poems Stink?

Why do my poems always stink?
Maybe I try too hard to think,
I try and try as hard as I can
But why do my poems always stink?

Sometimes I use strange words
For they always turn out quite absurd
I think and think and take my time
But never can make my poems rhyme

Why do my poems always stink?
That's it, I try too hard to think,
I think and think as hard as I can
But why do my poems always stink?

Glenn Stephens (11)
Finaghy Primary School

My Old School

I love my old school
Although it would be cool
If it had a big swimming pool
I would swim in it all night
Although the teachers in the morning
Might give me a fright

My new school will be cool
Even though it won't have a swimming pool
It will have a technology suite with lots of tools
I will use them all night
Although the teachers in the morning
Might give me a fright.

Nichola Luney (11)
Finaghy Primary School

My Sister

I have a beautiful sister,
Her name is Samantha Jane,
Her hair is golden brown
And her eyes, when they get angry,
Are shown with a frown.
Her radiant smile you can
See for a mile
As she grins
From cheek to cheek
She has spindly fingers
And legs that go on and on
Oh! How I wish that she could talk
And tell me what she's thinking
And when she starts her crying
She shows me what she's feeling
She's a very special person
A gift from God above
I'm very glad she is my sister,
As she surrounds me with her love.

Rebecca Mercer (9)
Finaghy Primary School

If My House Was A Zoo

Chimpanzee swings behind the TV
Bear sleeping on the chair
Otters sneak into the bath water
Snakes slither silently across the attic
Giraffe reaching to the roof
Lion lying lazily in the laundry
If my house was a zoo
I would snooze in my bed.

Rebekah Phelan (10)
Finaghy Primary School

The Cat And The Bat

There was a little woman
Who had a little cat
It sat on the mat
And she gave it a pat

There was a little woman
Who had a little bat
It hung on the wall
And sang to the cat

There was a little woman
Who loved her cat and bat
They loved to sing together
And have a little chat

There was a little woman
She loved to hear a rap
And gather all the letters
That were brought by Postman Pat.

Peter Ginn (8)
Finaghy Primary School

When Tilly Ate The Chilli

When Tilly ate the chilli,
It was piping hot.
When Tilly ate the chilli,
Her eyes began to pop.
When Tilly ate the chilli,
Her face came out in spots.
When Tilly ate the chilli,
It was hot, hot, hot!

Amanda Lillington (8)
Finaghy Primary School

My Family

My name is Zoë and I am very tall
My brother is very small
He wears a big nappy and he is very happy.

My family are funny
And they bake buns in bed.
My mum is funny,
Always when it is sunny.

Joe is mad
And I am glad,
But sometimes I can feel sad
When I do something bad.

Zoë Anderson (8)
Finaghy Primary School

My Mum

My mum laughs all day
She smiles at me when I do anything
She smiled when Erin threw a pie in the sky
My dad broke her favourite vase and she laughed
Then we got sick and tired of it
So we locked her in the cupboard but she still laughed
What will we do?
They said we need to hate her Sunday dinners
Put our feet up on the tables and if that doesn't work cry
So we tried it. Crying worked but we didn't like it
Because we got blamed for everything that broke.

Jade Marley (8)
Finaghy Primary School

Three Wishes

I wish, I wish I was a fish
Swimming out to sea
Cos then I'd have the ocean wide
To play in, just for me.

I wish, I wish I was a bird
Flying in the sky
Cos then I'd have the air so free
To soar in all the time.

I wish, I wish I was a snake
At night I'd catch my prey
Cos then I'd stretch out in the sun
And sleep the day away.

Owain Campton (9)
Finaghy Primary School

Food Poem

I like chips especially in garlic dip
Bread and butter is another that I like to eat as well
Washed down with a glass of Coke
I hope I don't get any stuck in my throat
Oh I hope I don't boak
I'm going to throw up in the sink
Oh I hope it doesn't stink.

Glenn Curtis McMillan (9)
Finaghy Primary School

Mr Cuddles

He sits very still on the window sill
Looking outside as on my bike I ride.
Wishing he could be with me
With his scarf and his hat and his belly so fat.
He looks ready to go, why is he so slow?
Why can he not be with me?
I can't wait anymore so I go through the door.
I rush up the stairs and I grab my teddy bear.
I gave him a snuggle because I love Mr Cuddles.
My favourite teddy bear will always be there.

Tara Gibney (9)
Finaghy Primary School

Puppy Poem

My family, we got a new puppy
It's a little brown and white Staffie
She's really so cute, so cuddly and smooth,
But sometimes she can be a bit waffy.
We take her for walks around the park,
When she sees another dog she starts to bark.
She's ever so small and she will never be tall
But I now she loves us all.
Her name is Cody and Cody is such a toady.

Aaron Hayes (8)
Finaghy Primary School

My Friends

I have a wee dolly called Molly,
Who has a friend called Solly.
I play with them in the sun ,
We go on holiday and have lots of fun.
When the sun goes down and it's time for bed,
I tuck them in beside my ted.

Sophie Dyer (9)
Finaghy Primary School

Actress

Loud speaker
Camera lover
Red carpet walker
Autograph signer
Movie master
Spotlight stander
Oscar winner
Hollywood happener
Star shiner.

Hannah Murray (11)
Finaghy Primary School

Kennings

Tooth poker,
Hole filler,
Tooth puller,
Brace fitter,
Sit back,
Open wide,
Who am I?

Ashton Higgins (10)
Finaghy Primary School

My Friend

Michael is my friend,
For him I'd like to lend,
My Ulster rugby ball
And give him a call,
To see if he'd like to play,
With me some Saturday.

Tom Matthews (9)
Finaghy Primary School

Walking

Walking up and down
Through the town
Walking so fast
It won't last.

Walking round the streets
Eating bags of sweets
Walking round the house
Found a happy mouse.

Walking in the room
It looks like a tomb
Walking up in space
Having a race.

Naomi Gribben (9)
Finaghy Primary School

Dentist

Decay killer
Tooth poker

Teeth whitener
Sweet killer

Gum stinger
Award is a sticker

Tooth keeper
Teeth lover

Hole filler
Tooth cleaner.

Joy Crockett (10)
Finaghy Primary School

Pile Driver

Noise maker
Brain wrecker
Earthquake maker
Puddle bouncer
Noisy machinery
Mad driver
Tile mover
Ear drummer
Ground smasher
Pile driver.

William McMillan (11)
Finaghy Primary School

If I Were A Frog

If I was a bright green frog
I'd sleep on a sunny log
And for a snack I'd eat a fly
Whenever one came buzzing by

I'd leap then swim in a pretty lake
And do frog things for goodness sake
It would be great but I suppose
That I would miss my spaghetti!

Hayley Anderson Traynor (9)
Finaghy Primary School

Mum

Mum oh Mum stop drying my clothes
Mum oh Mum stop smelling my toes
Mum oh Mum stop eating fresh meat
Mum oh Mum you tickle my feet
Mum oh Mum get the door I am asleep
Mum oh Mum goodnight my sweet.

Emma McFarland (10)
Finaghy Primary School

Dyspraxic Person

A ball dropper
A spelling mistake
A hard worker
A fast head
A slow hand
A hard thinker
A happy smile
A different person

Answer: dyspraxic person.

Ashleigh McCracken (10)
Finaghy Primary School

Waitress

Table setter
Food giver
Order taker
Bill leaver
Till opener
Table cleaner
Tray holder
Money maker.

Gemma Cleland
Finaghy Primary School

Lightning

The dark clouds drifting
The fierce lightning is frightening
The roaring thunder
Burning fiercely flashing forks
Destroying as it passes.

Andrew Moran (10)
Finaghy Primary School

Mechanic

Engine mender
Tyre repairer

Car fixer
Petrol checker

Forklift driver
Heavy loader

Exact designer
Vehicle driver

Break time worker
Heavy fixer.

Kyle Armstrong (10)
Finaghy Primary School

Hairdresser

Strange designer
Hairspray squirter

Water runner
Shampoo mixer

Edge snipper
Floor sweeper

Bobble collector
Scissor cleaner

Lolly giver
Tea drinker.

Carla Greeves (11)
Finaghy Primary School

Footballers

Penalty shooter
Free kicker

Brill defender
Star striker

Top midfielder
Goal scorer

League winners
Golden goal

Excellent manager
Super sub.

Rebecca Dallas (10)
Finaghy Primary School

Motorbike Racer

Noise maker
Body shaker

Fast rider
Sore seater

Big crasher
Dangerous racer

High jumper
Mountain climber

Man lover
Women hater.

Keith Copeland (10)
Finaghy Primary School

Astronaut

Blackness floater,
White-suit bloater.

Impossible jumper,
Brain stumper.

Space flyer,
High-in-skyer.

Moon walker,
Radio talker.

Crater explorer,
Float-off-floorer.

Johnathon Norman Mitchell (10)
Finaghy Primary School

Gardener

Green finger
Flower picker

Life giver
Pot planter

Help giver
Plant advisor

Late worker
Trowel buyer

Soil sorter
Greenhouse owner.

Jenni Uprichard (11)
Finaghy Primary School

Poem On Nature

Nature is pretty, nature is fun
With lovely colours that shine in the sun
From gold and red to white and green
Nature is really a sight to be seen.

In summer the sun shines high in the sky
And all the birds come out and fly
The trees are green and full of leaves
The flowers are blooming around the trees

In winter the wind is strong and cold
Woolly hats and gloves and mittens are sold
The children build snowmen and snowballs they throw
Until at last night comes and they go in from the snow

In autumn the leaves fall from the trees
The flowers soon will be dead
Until the season changes again
The colours will all turn red

The next season now has arrived
The trees and the flowers soon will regrow
The birds will return from their winter vacation
This season is spring and again round the nature cycle will go.

Rebekah Kirkwood (10)
Finaghy Primary School

Holidays

Holidays in the sun
Are so much fun,
When I jump into the pool
The water is so cool,
Oh, I love the feel of sand
On my hand.

Ciara Booth (10)
Gaelscoil Na Bhfál

Mummy Wrap!

There lived a king in Egyptian land
You know that place with piles of sand.
There was a king - Tutankhamun was his name.
I can't pronounce it, what a shame.
He's got a palace with piles of loot
He buys lots of pants for his elephants.
But even a king has to die,
So he took a drink, it smelt quite odd.
He shouldn't have taken that drink,
He should have poured it down the sink.
The king had died, his mates cried.
The servants cheered and Tut said nothing at all.
So King Tut slept for a thousand years,
Which is when our hero Mort appears.

James Murphy (9)
Gaelscoil Na Bhfál

A Spider The Size Of A Mouse

A spider the size of a mouse
Was running about my house.
Mummy said, 'You get out, out, out!'
The spider ran up the stairs.
Then he jumped on my toy bears.
I said, 'He's on my toy bear.'
It scared him.
He climbed up the wall
And fell on my toy ball.
Then Daddy kicked him out.

Kate Keenan (8)
Gaelscoil Na Bhfál

A Spider The Size Of A Mouse

A spider the size of a mouse
Is running about our house
He is frightening all the children
Who think he is as big as a hen

He's always walking about
With his two sharp teeth hanging out
His legs are as skinny as a stick
But his body is as fat as a brick
The mummy runs, jumps and shouts
(Get that spider out, out, out!)

He must have decided to go home
He started to wander and to roam
He tried the door at the back
It opened and closed and he got out
Just like that!

Lauren Morgan (10)
Gaelscoil Na Bhfál

A Spider The Size Of A Plane

A spider the size of a plane
Likes to sit and play games
He played too long
And turned into flames
And set his aim at David Blaine.
The spider was so big and
When he landed on a twig
He dug a hole then fell off a pole
But he thought it was a great big tower
He spun his web
Then thought he was a celeb.

Seosamh Lyons (11)
Gaelscoil Na Bhfál

A Spider The Size Of The Empire State

A spider the size of the Empire State
Honestly thought that he was quite great
Although he's really quite tall
We try to sneak by as he slumbers in the hall

When he jumps the floor shakes
He's now building a web of snakes
In which to trap flies of an enormous size
Now he'll have a fly feast
Oh what a prize!

The web is so thick
I can hardly see through it,
But the spider said
'There's really nothing to it'

The spider ran home all lonely and sad.
We finally got him out of our pad
We are glad to say goodbye to the spider the size
Of the Empire State, where he now lies.

Autumn McCullough (11)
Gaelscoil Na Bhfál

The Lady In The Park

I ran down the stairs
Because I heard the dog bark.
I let him out of the gate and he ran to the park.
I put on my coat and followed him down,
What in the world do you think that I found?
I found an old lady lying on the bench,
It started to rain and we both got drenched.
I picked up my dog and ran to the door,
Just as I got there I heard a bell ring,
Suddenly winter had turned into spring.

Nóirín Anne O'Neill (10)
Gaelscoil Na Bhfál

Our New Headmaster

Our new headmaster
Is called Mr Rocadile
He has a smile that's
A mile wide.

He beats you if you
Give him cheek with
His long and strong nose.

His favourite food is meat
With potatoes and leek.

When he's in bed and
If you go in and wake him up
He'll simply bite off your head.

Eibhleann Corbett (9)
Gaelscoil Na Bhfál

The Dark Wood

In the dark, dark wood
There was a dark, dark house
And in that dark, dark house
There was a room
And in that dark, dark room
There was a dark, dark cupboard
And in that dark, dark cupboard
There was a dark, dark shelf
And on that dark, dark shelf
There was a box
And in that dark, dark box
There was a . . . *ghost!*

Luke Robinson (9)
Gaelscoil Na Bhfál

My Sister

My sister is a little pest
But sometimes she can be the best.
Sometimes we're very good friends
But then again, we're not!

She can be funny all the time
But then sometimes, she can be weird!

She makes me stuff and I say thanks
And then she says 'It's a prank!'
I just want to say,
'Will you go to *Norway!*'

The other day she was sick
And I said, 'Get a grip!'
But in the end I love her lots
And I will buy her jelly tots!

Niamh Taylor (10)
Gaelscoil Na Bhfál

Annoying Little Sister

My sister is so annoying
She makes me wanna scream
She makes me wanna lift her head
And shove it into cream
When I annoy my sister
She swells up like a blister
But when she annoys me
She makes me wanna run away
But I will get her back
Some day, some day, some day.

David Nelson (10)
Gaelscoil Na Bhfál

Are All The Giants Dead?

Are all the giants dead?
And all the witches fled?
Am I quite safe in bed?
Giants and witches are all fled

My child, you are quite safe in bed
I don't believe my mother,
I know there is another,
Somewhere, out there, anywhere, everywhere,
They could be in the mountains
They could be in the fountains
Somewhere, out there, anywhere, everywhere
Spooky, creepy, supernatural beings
With no kind or caring feelings

Giants, witches
When they're near I get itches.
Vampires, ghosts are the ones I hate the most.
Werewolves, goblins when they're near
I get the woblins.
Bats and rats I whack them with bats
Whack, smack, crack!
Bam, slam, sock!

Spooky, pukey
With ugly nuglies,
They make me shake and quake.

I'm feeling scared of bugs
Hiding under the rugs
I kiss a four-leaved clover
And a rabbit's foot named Rover,
Throw salt over my shoulder,
To help me get over.

And hang garlic on my bed
So that when I wake up
There won't be two bite marks
On my neck
That are the colour red.

Some silver round my neck
So when I wake there won't be
A monster hair down my throat
That will make me choke

And a bucket of water,
For the witch to knock over.

And some dust on the table
With a missing stable
For the mummy to trip
And rip
And the dust will make him rust
And die
And I'll give him to my mum,
To bake and make into pie.

So the big question is . . .
Are all the giants dead?
Are all the witches fled?
Am I quite safe in bed?
May the Lord help me
For I'm going to die
In my jammies
Help me I need to live this night,
So I won't die of fright.
I need a cross
And a dummy
And red sauce to fool a ghoul
I need to live this night
I need to live this night
I am only three years old.

Turlough Lavery (8)
Gaelscoil Na Bhfál

My Special Nanny

My nanny's name is Eileen.
I love her so much,
I would give her my life to keep her alive.
She is so sick.
She takes lots of tablets.
She has a machine to keep her going.
I live with her.
I always watch that she's OK.
I make her tea and toast.
I pray for her to live forever,
Like a ghost.
I clean, I give her a hand,
I make sure she takes her medicine.
When I'm going somewhere
I give her a kiss and a hug
And always say goodbye.

Liam McMahon (10)
Gaelscoil Na Bhfál

My Dog Claira

My dog is called Claira
Her coat is tan and white
She chases me round the house
And gives me a fright
She barks at me every night
To see the tricks she does
They are funny
She likes a scratch when we are in bed
When I feel asleep
She was licking my head.

Aoibh McLaughlin (8)
Gaelscoil Na Bhfál

My Great Granda Paddy

My great granda loves his pigeons.
He'd call them back at night.
He'd whistle for old Toby to come in
And say, 'Good morning Toby,' and then come in.
He always chased me around the table
Until I laughed so hard my face went purple,
But I was only two then.
A couple of weeks went by and poor old Toby died.
My granda Paddy was heartbroken.
Granda Paddy got very sick.
He had to give the pigeons away because the dust infected his lungs.
When I was nine he was dying,
I felt very, very sad.
I went to his house with my mum.
He died right in front of me.
He took his last breath and the light faded.
I was crying and crying my heart out.
Granny Vera just stared.
My granny Vera died five weeks later at 12 o'clock at night.
But I'm happy I was there to say goodbye.
I miss them very much.

Emma McDonald (10)
Gaelscoil Na Bhfál

My Baby Cousin

I like my baby cousin,
He is very funny.
Once he got a little dog
And shook it like a bunny
And when it is bedtime,
He screams all night.
Then in the morning,
There is a fight.

Lee McCann (9)
Gaelscoil Na Bhfál

My Great Granny

My great granny was as funny as a bunny,
I love her so much,
When she went out shopping,
I would go trotting,
On my wee pink horse,
We would eat ice cream and scream,
We loved it all the time,
Then one day she told me
She'd pass away and then one day
She did pass away and I was
So sad I cried all day because I love her,
So much and I still remember her.

Fionnghuala Higgins (9)
Gaelscoil Na Bhfál

Dentist

Death to that dentist of mine.
He hurts my gums and teeth.
Death to that nurse of his.
She gives me pink water to spit out (euch).
Oh it's horrible, I hate it so much.
I know he's there to keep my teeth white and clean,
But I hate 'open wide please'.
I hate the drill and the glass mirror.

I wonder do I really hate him
Or am I just scared?

Patrice Kelly (10)
Gaelscoil Na Bhfál

Being The Youngest

Why couldn't I be born first?
It's just not fair.
My two older brothers
Are always pulling my hair.

I have to go to bed early,
Everyone teases me,
Every night I say,
'I'll get you back - you'll see!'

When they're talking about something secret and important,
I have to go out of the room.
You don't get as much food
And you get the smallest bedroom.

If they're planning a surprise for someone,
You're not allowed to know.
If you ask for money,
They always say no.

Oh, I wish I could be the oldest,
I could drink alcohol and wine.
I could drive the car wherever I want
Wouldn't that be just fine.

I could boss my little brothers about,
I wouldn't have to go to mass.
I think that being the oldest,
Would definitely be first class!

Megan Weir (9)
Gaelscoil Na Bhfál

A Spider The Size Of Barney

A spider the size of Barney
Liked to fight with Marty
One day he got a grip and
Started to kick
But Marty was stronger and
Hit him with a brick

He started to run
But was injured by a gun
Which hurt his lung
He went to emergency
And had to have surgery
He thought it was awful
When he had his fill
Was given a pill
Then rang his friend Bill.

Clíodhna Morrison (11)
Gaelscoil Na Bhfál

Fright

In the middle of the night
I woke with a fright
I jumped when I heard snapping and growling
Buster my dog was barking and howling
I crept down the stairs not wanting to see
A burglar standing there, waiting for me
I went to the cupboard and picked up a bat
I ran in to face him but slipped on a mat
My bum was sore and my head was aching
As I lay on the floor shivering and shaking
I stared at the hall you can imagine my reaction
My stupid dog was barking, at his own reflection.

Pádraig McBride (10)
Gaelscoil Na Bhfál

A Spider The Size Of A Head

A spider the size of a head,
Found a woman in bed.
He crawled up beside her, drenched her in cider,
Then she looked a whole lot brighter.

After a week it grew 50 feet,
Now it's as large as a field of wheat.
It had built three webs made out of heads
With hair dangling from them.
It grew again to the size of Spain
And now it's eating the world.

But then with lots of luck
It fell into the muck
And he then started to cluck,
'Help me please, I'm sticking,
And I've turned into a chicken!'

Paul Nolan (11)
Gaelscoil Na Bhfál

A Spider The Size Of A House

A spider the size of a house
Who liked to play with a mouse
Put up a trap
And started to rap

While he was rapping
He heard someone clapping
'What is it?' he said
'I want to go to bed!'

When he stopped rapping
That someone stopped clapping
And started to shout
'Help me get out!'

Sinead Campbell (11)
Gaelscoil Na Bhfál

A Spider The Size Of A Balloon

On a dark, cold night
With no one in sight
Just me and my teddy in bed,
From the corner of my eye
What did I spy?
'Oh my God,' I nearly dropped dead.

There on the wall
It made my skin crawl
Was a spider the size of a balloon.
With no one else there
I felt really scared
My only comfort being the light from the moon.

I crept out of bed
All thoughts in my head
Of that monster on the wall.
I turned on the light
And there on my right
Was a spider half an inch tall.

Then to my delight
What gave me the fright
Was a spider the size of a crumb.
It was the light from the moon
That made it look gloom
Now I'm happy alone in my room.

Niamh Burns (11)
Gaelscoil Na Bhfál

A Spider The Size Of My Finger

A spider the size of my finger
Who thinks he's a really great swinger
Has feet the size of a metre
Wouldn't he make a brilliant leader!

His claws are the size of a rat
When I saw him I ran for my bat
He quickly ran away and hid
But then I hit him under the bin lid.
I hit him on the head
Until he was dead.
Poor, poor, Fred!

Jim O'Hanlon (10)
Gaelscoil Na Bhfál

The Warrior's Ballad

As around him the battle raged on,
He sang his true but saddening song.
Of triumph and victory,
Injuries and death,
Of brave men dying
For homeland and wealth.

Dropping his defence he carried on;
Singing of courageous men in battle,
Simple peasants and their cattle.
The world around us we live in,
The world around us filled with sin.

An arrow sped through the air.
Did anyone care?
As the brave man fell to the ground,
Uttering one last sound . . .
Did we win?

Elizabeth Murphy (10)
Holy Rosary Primary School

Questions And Answers

Why do stars come out at night?
It is too bright at daytime.
Why are chicks yellow?
The sun yellowed them.
Why is Wednesday called that?
People get married on that day.
Why do trees love autumn?
They lose their kids and have another lot after!
Why do we cry?
Because people cut onions.
Why do we have spring?
So lambs can be born, hens eat corn.
Why do we have summer?
So we can hear children play on a hot summer's night.
Why does winter come?
So Santa can appear on Christmas night!

Sarah McGrenaghan (11)
Holy Rosary Primary School

Questions And Answers

Who made the Earth?
God made the Earth.
Who was the first person on the moon?
Neil Armstrong.
Why was the Earth made?
So humans could live on Earth.
Why were humans made?
So we could face facts of life.
Why were we taught to work?
So we could learn things.
Why were we given names?
So we would not get mixed up by different people!

Emma Moreland (10)
Holy Rosary Primary School

Questions And Answers

What's inside the moon?
White cheese.
Who shot the first gun?
The person who pulled the trigger and lay on the ground.
Who discovered gravity?
Someone who was hit on the head with an apple.
Why do people kill animals?
They are selfish.
What was the first living thing to touch a book?
A bookworm.

Paul Stelges (11)
Holy Rosary Primary School

The Colour Of War

Fiercesome dragons flying through the sky
Raging bulls, charging 'cross the land
Fierce, fighting ants fighting bravely in the sand.
Roaring lions with tongues of flame
Cunning rattlesnakes with a tail of death
And sleek, swift hawks with a head of terror
Bringing fear, destruction and death.

Conall Bailie (11)
Holy Rosary Primary School

Love

Love is sweet like sugar and spice
Love smells like a beautiful, scented rose
Tastes like red juicy strawberries
Sounds like a romantic night with birds singing quietly
Feels like ovules in the palm of a flower
Like love in the middle of my hand
Looks like a beautiful field of scented poppies and lilies.

Lauren Little (11)
Holy Rosary Primary School

My Family

On Monday Mum baked a casserole
She used a *How To Make A Chair* book
I wish she had taken a better look
Screws and nuts aren't as tasty
As fluffy, brown pastry.

On Tuesday Dad drove us to school
He thought he looked very cool
Only problem was -
He wore a tie, hat and coat
But forgot the rest of his clothes.

On Wednesday I insisted
We walk to school ourselves
Unfortunately my brother
Misplaced his glasses -
He mistook me for a gerbil
When he said to some lasses -
'Look at my pet gerbil,'
They gave him a look.

Thursday, my aunt pretended
To be Captain Hook
At school assembly she rushed in
With cutlass and all
And told the principal to -
'Walk the plank!'

On Friday my uncle Hank
Took me to the cinema
He snored all through the movie
And shouted in his sleep!
I covered my face
And didn't dare peep.

So you see my family
Are a joy to have around -
If you block out
Sight and sound.

Louise McLaughlin (11)
Holy Rosary Primary School

Hallowe'en

Did I hear a swish of a vampire's cape?
No, just the wind down by the lake.
Did I hear a howl of a wolf?
No, just my dog, 'Woof, woof!'

Did I smell the smell of blood?
No, just our soup which tastes like mud!
Did I smell the smell of hate?
No, just my brother in a state!

Have I felt something strange in the air?
Why does that sign read *Beware*?
Something weird is here tonight -
It's going to give us all a fright!

Laura Curry (10)
Holy Rosary Primary School

Haikus

The eagle soars high
Searching around for its food
Ready to attack.

The Viking boat sails
Across the rough seas again
Bringing Vikings home.

Paul Maguire Wilson (10)
Holy Rosary Primary School

Midnight Haiku

Midnight is a place
When people go joyriding
Dark and spooky night.

Glenn King (11)
Holy Rosary Primary School

Bully

I hate the way you leave me out
I hate the way you mess me about
But most of all -
I hate the way you kick me about.

I hate the way you steal my money
I hate the way you make fun of my mummy
I hate the way you bully me
Oh please God
Set me free!
You make me miserable
Please - just stop
I hate this!

Conor Stewart (11)
Holy Rosary Primary School

Alarm Clock

Beep . . . beep . . . beep
I am fast asleep
Beep . . . beep . . . beep
It took me ages to get to sleep
Beep . . . beep . . . beep
Counting all those bloomin' sheep!
Time to get up and start -
A new day -
When all I want to do
Is stay
In bed!

Anna Carr (11)
Holy Rosary Primary School

Love

Love is strawberry-red
Tastes like lemon pie
Feels like the sea spraying my face
Smells like baking in the kitchen
Looks like a red sky at noon
Love is flying high in the clouds.

Bebhinn Schaible (10)
Holy Rosary Primary School

Limerick

There was an old man from Tyrone
Who sang his name down the phone
It might have been quiet
But it still caused a riot
That quiet old man from Tyrone.

Daniel Robinson (10)
Holy Rosary Primary School

Wonderland

Wonder
Wonder
Wonderland
What does it look like?
Where does it stand?

I think I know where your wonderland stands,
Far, far away in a faraway land.

Rebecca McKee (10)
Knockbreda Primary School

Winter's Here

When it's cold outside
And the strings on your coat are all tied,
You know winter's here.

When the cold goes down your pants
And you look on the ground and there's no ants,
You know winter's here.

When Jack Frost knocks at your door
And it's too cold to put your feet on the floor,
You know winter's here.

When your nose turns bright red
And you just want to snuggle in bed,
You know winter's here.

Kyle Dugan (9)
Knockbreda Primary School

Winter

Cloud and rain and long, dark nights,
Feeling cold and shivery, needing lots of light,
Coming in early, no time to play,
Oh how I wish for a summer's day!
Cold, icy winds bringing snow,
Snowmen, snowball fights, out we go!
Freezing water, making ice rinks in the yard,
Skating, sliding, falling down hard,
Cosy coal fires lit at night,
Wooden logs burning bright,
Oh how I love a winter's night!

Philip Davison (9)
Knockbreda Primary School

Spooky

(Based on 'The Door' by Miroslav Holub)

Go and open the door,
Maybe there'll be an Orc
Or a mummy

Go and open the door,
Maybe there's an alien
Or killer bees
Or Darth Maul

Go and open the door,
Maybe it's Jack the Ripper
Or Long John Silver
Maybe it's Nick Nack or Jaws
Or Odd-Job

Go and open the door,
Is it the man with no name
Or the Grim Reaper?
Or it might be . . . Granny!

James Connery (10)
Knockbreda Primary School

Don't Eat Me

Don't eat me, don't eat me, I'm just a tiny crumb,
I don't think I'm tasty or I don't think I'm yum,
Oh help me, oh help I must want my mum,
Wouldn't you rather just suck your thumb?

Please go away and leave me be
Can't you see, oh can't you see
It's not fair to pick on me?
Just go away and leave me be.

Niamh Weir (9)
Knockbreda Primary School

The Door

(Based on 'The Door' by Miroslav Holub)

Go and open the door
A spider might be there
If there is don't let it bite
Or else you'll not be there

Go and open the door
And open it again
If you hear a clucking
It's sure to be a hen

Go and open the door
You don't know what you'll find
A whisker, a flea
But I don't really mind
You might see a rugby ball
Or a golf tee

Go and open the door
If you're lucky it might snow
You might have to do hard sums
Oh no!

Luke McCann (9)
Knockbreda Primary School

Eating Potatoes

Peppers are red,
Blueberries are blue,
Potatoes are sweet,
Especially in stew.
I eat them boiled,
I eat them mashed,
I eat them very, very fast.

Victoria Carson (8) & Christine Collins (9)
Knockbreda Primary School

The Potato's Stages

I'm a potato,
Deep in the ground,
Spring is coming near,
So I think I'll be found.

I'm a potato picked and in a pot,
I'm going to be a boiled potato,
Hot, hot, hot.

I'm a boiled potato,
Cooked and on a plate,
Help, the fork is coming,
What will be my fate?

Stuart Lammey (10)
Knockbreda Primary School

Autumn Leaves

Down
They
Flow
Faster and faster
Curling and twirling.
Flying berries dribbling
Down through
Gingers and
Browns.
Oozing and oozing
Nearer the ground.

John Lynn (10)
Knockbreda Primary School

How I Got Eaten

I am a potato
I've travelled the world.
When I got to Ireland
I found it was quite weird.
They cooked me and washed me
And gave me to a cook.
Then I ended up
In her potato soup.

Matthew Deane (9)
Knockbreda Primary School

City Nights

C ity lights in the middle of the night
I like the lights they are so bright
T urn your car lights on or you might have a crash
Y oung kids have to go to bed early at night.

N ight-time is a bright time
I am sometimes bored at night when my friends are in bed asleep
G o to work at night or you will not get any money
H appy people don't make any noise at night
T alk quietly because everyone likes to have a good night's sleep
S ome people don't like night shift because it is very hard work.

Jonathan Goddard (10)
Malvern Primary School

Winter

When it is winter it snows
Sometimes people make snowmen
Winter is in January and December
Sometimes people get cold in winter.

Courtney Cinnamon (8)
Malvern Primary School

City Nights

C ity nights are cold and bare
I n the cold and frosty air
T he tall buildings and shining lights
Y ou look around and get a fright.

N ow it feels as if it's going to rain
I think my mum is such a pain
G oing back to my home at last
H ome I get warm and fast
T onight my feelings were tired and upset
S o look at me I'm awfully wet.

Shannon Brownlee (9)
Malvern Primary School

Smoking

S moking is bad for your lungs
M illions of people die from lung cancer
O rgans will be destroyed
K ills you and destroys you
I f I was you I wouldn't smoke
N ever smoke because it gives you cancer
G as is in cigarettes and tar.

Ashleigh Gaynor (9)
Malvern Primary School

Winter

W inter is cold
I started to put my hat on
N early always when it's cold you get sick
T o put your hat and scarf on
E at your dinner and go out - it's cold
R ain comes in winter.

Cody McMillan (8)
Malvern Primary School

City Nights

C ity nights, lights shining bright
I n the darkness I sometimes get a fright
T raffic rushing in the night
Y oung children walking by the street lights.

N ot very warm walking home
I n the darkness all alone
G oing home to go to bed
H uge buildings above my head
T ired I am, but I'll be home soon
S hining above me the big, bright moon.

Philip Morrison (9)
Malvern Primary School

Smoking

S moking damages your lungs
M y uncle Sammy stopped smoking five years ago
        but my auntie has not
O rgans in your body do not like smoke
K eep smoking and you will damage your health
I do not like breathing in smoke
N ever start smoking just because your friends do
G iving up smoking is hard because of the nicotine in cigarettes.

Craig Harrison (9)
Malvern Primary School

Autumn

A utumn leaves come down from the trees
U nder the leaves the hedgehogs sleep
T he leaves crunch under your feet
U mbrellas keep you dry
M ist covers the hillside
N uts are eaten by squirrels.

Nicole McDowell (8)
Malvern Primary School

City Nights

C ity nights, you can hear the cars going home
I n the bin the cats get food
T he people from offices turn the lights off at midnight
Y ou can hear the music blasting from the cars.

N ights get dark very quickly
I can see a shooting star
G irls and boys go out to play when the sky is going grey
H ungry people coming home
T onight I feel very lonely
S o lonely.

Megan Hollyoak (9)
Malvern Primary School

Smoking

S moking is expensive
M any people smoke and they die
O xygen is reduced
K ills lots of people
I t smells horrible
N icotine is addictive
G as and tar.

William Morton (9)
Malvern Primary School

Smoking

S ome smoke is very poisonous
M akes you ill
O rgans will be destroyed
K ills people every day
I am *never* going to smoke
N icotine is in a cigarette
G ives you cancer.

Kyle Morton (9)
Malvern Primary School

Winter

W inter is very cold
I ce can make you slip
N ever walk on ice
T ry not to fall on ice
E verybody slips on ice
R emember to wear your hat and scarf.

Natasha Haveron (7)
Malvern Primary School

Snow

S ometimes it snows
N ow it is cold
O n winter nights it is freezing
W hen you get a coat on it is warmer.

Jonathan McCallion (8)
Malvern Primary School

Snow

S now is cold
N o one likes snow
O n we put our coats and hats
W inter is cold.

Aaron Patterson (8)
Malvern Primary School

Snow

S now is white and cold
N o dogs like snow
O n go the coats and hats
W inter is cold.

Jordan McAuley (8)
Malvern Primary School

Autumn

A lot of birds fly to warmer countries
U nder the water frogs hibernate
T he weather is wet and windy
U nder my feet leaves crunch
M isty mornings are cold
N ext is winter.

Curtis Griffiths (8)
Malvern Primary School

Cold

C hocolate calendars go up
O n go the hats and scarves
L ittle children play in the cold
D ecorations all around.

Jemma McKittrick (7)
Malvern Primary School

Snow

S mall things in the sky
N ever here when it's hot
O h snow is good
W hite snow is all around.

Daniel Fisher (7)
Malvern Primary School

Cold

C old is in the air
O nce kids are out they are freezing
L ittle kids love the cold
D ogs hate the cold.

Connor Irvine (8)
Malvern Primary School

My Dog Scampi

Long curly hair
like a sheepdog

He is black
and white
like a TV in the olden days

His tail wags
like birds' wings
in the sky

As skinny as
a lamp post

Dark brown eyes
like chocolate

He has a sad face
like a robin.

Sarah Wilkinson (8)
Mersey Street Primary School

Autumn

Leaves are falling on the ground
Orange and brown
Orange and brown
Leaves are falling on the ground
On the ground orange and brown

Autumn is so colourful
Delicious red berries
Delicious red berries
Autumn is so colourful
It is my favourite season of the year.

Taylor Gray (8)
Mersey Street Primary School

The Writer Of This Poem

(Based on 'The Writer Of This Poem' by Roger McGough)

The writer of this poem
Is as tough as bricks
As sharp as a pin
As smart as a Smartie.

As fast as a car
As slick as a snake
As cool as an ice cube
As great as a win.

Edmund Green (11)
Mersey Street Primary School

Hallowe'en

H is for horror on Hallowe'en night where all the people have fun.
A is for apples that everybody eats.
L is for fireworks that light up the sky.
L is for all the laughing on Hallowe'en night.
O is for *oooh*, the sounds that ghosts make.
W is for werewolves on Hallowe'en!
E is for everyone who plays and has fun.
E is for evil people on Hallowe'en who scare us.
N is for the noisy, crackling fireworks.

Samuel Conlane (10)
Mersey Street Primary School

Snowy Days

Snowy days are fun
But you can't run
You can build snowmen
Sometimes it is icy
Some people slide on the ice.

Adam Swain (9)
Mersey Street Primary School

Hallowe'en

H is for haunted house where we die!
A is for *aaah* when ghosts come to kill.
L is for lightning, the fireworks in the sky.
L is for laughing witches at Hallowe'en.
O is for *ooh,* that the ghosts try to scare me with.
W is for werewolves in the deep, dark forests.
E is for echoes when people get chased by ghosts.
E is for evilness that goes on in dark places.
N is for nasty when witches are behind killing others.

Dean Proctor (10)
Mersey Street Primary School

My Viking Poem

V is for victory they often got in battles.
I is for the innocent people they killed!
K is for killing, because that's what they were good at.
I is for Iceland where the brutal Vikings lived.
N is for nasty, because they were always nasty to others!
G is for great, as they thought they were after battles they won!
S is for the slaughtering they did in battles!

Nicole Palmer (10)
Mersey Street Primary School

Bullies

B is for blackmail they threaten you with
U is for upset victims that bullies hurt
L is for losers, that's what the bullies are
L is for losing the lunch money that the bullies take
I is for the innocent victims that bullies hurt
E is for their evil laughing at victims
S is for sorry that the bullies can never say.

Ryan Giltrap (9)
Mersey Street Primary School

Hallowe'en

H is for the horrible witches that fly in the night.
A is for the apples that children duck for.
L is for the laughing children when it's Hallowe'en.
L is for the fireworks that light up in the sky.
O is for the noise ghosts make - *ooh!*
W is for the witches and the wizards that fly around the sky.
E is for everyone that is dressed up.
E is for eating that the children do, gobbling lots of food.
N is for the noisy children that go around doors trick or treating.

Sarah-Louise Laverty (9)
Mersey Street Primary School

Bullies

B is for broken hearts of the victims
U is for the unhappy people every day who get bullied
L is for the laughing of the bully every day
L is for the losing of the victim in a fight
I is for the illness of the victim every morning
E is for the evilness of the bully
S is for sorry, that is the hardest word for a bully to say.

Martin Kemp (10)
Mersey Street Primary School

Viking Poem

V is for how violent the Vikings were in battles.
I is for Iceland, one of the many countries they came from.
K is for killings they did for pleasure.
I is for the innocent people they killed out of joy and cruelty.
N is for the nastiness they inherited.
G is for the great fighters they were
S is for the slaughtering they did on their raids.

Alan Fisher (9)
Mersey Street Primary School

Splashing Waves

The waves start at dawn
They go on and on
They smash and they crash
They splash and they crash

The waves go high
Not as high as the sky
They are blue
It is true

They are tall
They are not small
They go on all day
They don't stop the whole way.

Luke Wilson (9)
Mersey Street Primary School

Viking Poem

V is for the victory that the Vikings got in every fight
I is for the innocent people that the Vikings killed
K is for the evil killers, that's what the Vikings were
I is for Ireland that's where the Vikings lived
N is for the nastiness that the Vikings possessed
G is for our gangsters today, they are like Vikings
S is for the slaves that they brought with them to treat badly.

Curtis Wynne (10)
Mersey Street Primary School

A Love Poem

Two lovers stood on London Bridge
He kissed her cheek
And he felt weak and fell into the river
And he came out in a quiver
And never went to it again.

Aaron Clarke (10)
Mersey Street Primary School

Night-Time

I spy with my wondering eye,
How those stars sparkle,
So high up in that black sky,
How could I know it is not a show?
I saw a sparkling star go by
What was it? I didn't know!
A shooting star or
Just a normal star,
Shining brightly?
The stars in that dark
Black ebony sky,
They sprinkle out
Love to me,
I drift away peacefully!

Melissa Seawright (8)
St Bernadette's Primary School, Ballymurphy

The Night

The kitten runs and pounces on me
As I frolic for the last time at night
I go and pull my curtains over
And look at Heaven's light,
The stars show Heaven's dazzle
Golden, blackened sky,
Oh what a sight!
As I climb into bed
I think of people that are dead
I wonder at this starry night
I hope it will keep them safe this night
The kitten watches with me too
Because that's what it likes to do.

Sara Louise Murphy (9)
St Bernadette's Primary School, Ballymurphy

Night-Time

I lie in bed at night-time
Still not asleep
I go to the window
The sun starts to weep
In my peace and serenity
I take a look outside
My thoughts start to flow
Stars might enchant you
They make time stand still
They give me a wish high above
Leave me at their will
I say goodbye to the afternoon
My eyes open wide
The memories that are in my little life
Are locked safe inside.

Kerry Stone (8)
St Bernadette's Primary School, Ballymurphy

Worm

Spaghetti
    like
slime
    skipping rope
wriggling
    through
the soil
    ground-
eater
    fish-
baiter
    birds'
food!

Danielle McKnight (9)
St Bernadette's Primary School, Ballymurphy

Bedtime

As I look out my window,
I see the moonlight shine,
I see the stars twinkling up
In that everlasting sky.
As I look over the side of them,
I see the big white moon.
I look over at the stars again
And dream they will be back soon.
I talk to God up so high
And thank Him for my day.
I close my eyes for a gentle dream
And let the great day fade away.
I dream of things like cats and dogs
But nothing much to do
When I have deep dream I always think of you
In other dreams I think of people that have died all year
When I go to bed I always have a fear.

Megan O'Hare (9)
St Bernadette's Primary School, Ballymurphy

The Stars

As I lay on my bed,
Watching the world go by,
I think of all the people who have died
When I see the stars I think,
I wish I could turn back time
To see them again
And then I feel they're back again.

Jamie Wallace (9)
St Bernadette's Primary School, Ballymurphy

Night-Time

When I looked out my bedroom window,
The stars twinkled with golden tips.
I could see the yellow moon,
Shrouded in the cloudy velvet sky.
Then a shooting star goes racing by.
I can feel my hot water bottle.
I forget about today.
I think about the next one
And I gently close my eyes
Till today fades away.
One last look at the stars
Inspires my dreams tonight.
I feel myself drifting to faraway lands,
Today is now far out of sight.

Lauren Clarke (9)
St Bernadette's Primary School, Ballymurphy

At Night

As I lay my head to the pillow
moonlight gleams across my face
I watch the stars above the world
and the planets high,
Saturn, Jupiter, Mars, Pluto, Venus,
and the one we live on, Earth.
I like Mars to see with a telescope
beside the sun, the hottest one.
Pluto is further away, the coldest one,
in the Universe you take one breath
you freeze your lungs and fall down dead.

Danielle O'Donoghue (8)
St Bernadette's Primary School, Ballymurphy

Night-Time

While I am in bed listening to sounds,
I think of the day that's coming around,
I look at the stars glistening, the moonlight too!
When I look at them all I think only of you.

I spy with wondering eye
The shimmering stars above,
How I'd love to touch them,
If only I could!

As the night drifts in,
Today becomes yesterday,
The stars take me to my dream
Watching over me where I lay.

Kerry-Ann Rainey (9)
St Bernadette's Primary School, Ballymurphy

The Giraffe

If I were a giraffe
Long and tall
I'd like to jump
Over a wall.
If I were a giraffe
Long and tall
I'd ski down a mountain
And pray I don't fall.
If I were a giraffe
Long and tall
I'd play games of football
And win them all.

Kirsty Hughes (9)
St Bernadette's Primary School, Ballymurphy

Night-Time

When I go to the starlit window,
I hear lots of people,
Banging, slamming and shouting,
But I don't care!

When I go to the starlit window,
I see lots of things,
Lights, traffic, people too,
But I don't care!

When I am in my soft little bed,
I think of people that are dead,
And think of Heaven in each little star,
And I do care.

I wonder are you cold up so high?
I think of you among the glistening stars,
But I leave them in their twinkling light,
Goodnight! Goodnight!
I do care, I do care!

Samantha Morgan (9)
St Bernadette's Primary School, Ballymurphy

Night-Time

As I look out my window
A star sits above my tree
And when I am sitting in my bed
The star sits and looks at me.
I went to look out my window
And I was reading my book
I thought the star said
'I want to sit with you'
But soon I had fallen asleep.

Lauren Hyland (9)
St Bernadette's Primary School, Ballymurphy

Young Writers - Once Upon A Rhyme Belfast

My Weird Dream

I had a weird dream,
It was about me,
Sitting on the clouds,
Listening to Girls Aloud.

I was singing and dancing,
When something came upon me,
It was the stars,
And they were coming from Mars,
But then my dream went away.

So I woke up,
And went to school,
I told my mates,
And they thought I was a fool.

Seaneen O'Hara (11)
St Catherine's Primary School, Belfast

My Imaginary Friend

I have an imaginary friend,
Who drives me round the bend.
I try to tell him to be quiet,
But he just talks on and doesn't buy it.

My mum thinks I'm a bit mad,
But I am very glad,
Because if I was bad,
I would blame it on Brad.

Brad is very sad,
Because my mum thinks he's bad,
But now he's really glad,
Because he's liked by my dad.

Courtney Di Lucia (10)
St Catherine's Primary School, Belfast

Special People

I have special people
They love me with all their heart
They live all over the world
On a certain day every year
They send me a piece
of love
And on other days too
They help me with lots of homework
including problems
They make me better when I am hurt
or sick
They love me just the way I am
Because they are my
family.

Rachael McLean (10)
St Catherine's Primary School, Belfast

The Wonderful Dream

There it was in front of me,
The biggest sweet in the world,
With stripes and dots
And lovely swirls.
All the children were amazed
Just to see that huge, wonderful gaze.
The sun was shining bright and hot
For that special sweet
In the street.

Elisha Black (10)
St Catherine's Primary School, Belfast

Best Friends

Best friends care for you
Best friends never die
Best friends are always there for you
Best friends are like a pot of gold
Best friends share with you
Best friends are like a heart that never breaks
Best friends never fight with you
Best friends never walk away from you
Best friends never tut

If you were me
You'd be lucky
to have a best friend like
Mine.

Zoe Burns (10)
St Catherine's Primary School, Belfast

Speedy

I have a pet monkey,
He eats bananas all day,
He makes a mess of our house,
Mum wants me to give him away.

I call him Speedy,
Because he is fast,
Any time he races,
He never comes last.

I will never give him away,
He is too special to me,
Mum will just have to get used to him,
She'll love him you see!

Rebecca Ainsworth (10)
St Catherine's Primary School, Belfast

Why?

I'm just going out for a moment.
Why?
To make a cup of tea.
Why?
Because I'm thirsty.
Why?
Because it's hot.
Why?
Because the sun is shining.
Why?
Because it's summer.
Why?
Because she's talking on the phone.
Why?
Because she's very bossy.
Why?
Why won't you stop saying 'Why?'
Why?

Rebecca McCormick (8)
St Catherine's Primary School, Belfast

Daisy And Maisy

I have a dog called Daisy
She is very lazy.
I tell her to do tricks
But my hand she just licks.
I like Daisy
I know she is lazy
But she is funny
And a brown colour.
I like Daisy
She is just like my dog Maisy.

Bronagh O'Prey (10)
St Catherine's Primary School, Belfast

The Fairy Princess

Fairies are a fairy tale, they say,
I believe them anyway!

Once upon a time,
Beside a little rose bush,
I met the fairy princess,
She was called Nush.

She told me her secrets,
I told her mine.
Then she brought me
To the secret vine.

Finally we had to say goodbye,
'Will you be back again?' I said,
She said, 'I'll try!'

Megan McBride (9)
St Catherine's Primary School, Belfast

The Best Brother

I have a baby brother
He's one year old
Sometimes he can be grisly
But he's my pot of gold.

His eyes are like the ocean
He has a button nose.
He likes to play with his rattle and me
I bounce him on my knee
While I tell him nursery rhymes.

Stephanie McKeown (11)
St Catherine's Primary School, Belfast

Dream Of Death

I had a dream last night
While I was asleep in my bed
I didn't know what it meant
The vision I had in my head.

I saw a young woman
On top of a cliff
She didn't say a word
Just stood there stiff.

She turned and stared at me
Her complexion pale and sad
Her face it told a tale
Of the kin she never had

She took a step forward
Let out a cry
And like a crow
Her black dress flies.

As I look over the cliff
The silence that descends
Is it a dream or not?
Will my nightmare ever end?

Maureen Turner (10)
St Catherine's Primary School, Belfast

Best Friends

A best friend is someone who never lets you down
A best friend is someone who plays with you all day long
A best friend is someone who never goes behind your back
A best friend is someone who never talks about you.

Jolene Ann McFarlane (10)
St Catherine's Primary School, Belfast

I'm Going To The Shoe Shop Now

I'm going to the shoe shop now.
Why?
To get new shoes!
Why?
Because if I don't get new shoes everyone will die.
Why?
Because my feet reek.
Why?
Because I have not washed them in three years.
Why?
Because I'm too lazy.
Why?
Oh, but I'm not too lazy to kill you.
Why?
Because you've a heck of a nerve. Shut up saying 'Why!'
Why?
I'm going to the hospital.
Why?
To get you brain surgery to stop saying 'Why!'
Why?
Come on let's go.
When?

Laurie-Ann Mary Bartsch (9)
St Catherine's Primary School, Belfast

The Jungle

Come with me to the jungle tonight
Don't take a big fright
See the spiders
See the lions
Come to see the big tigers . . .

Just come to the jungle tonight!

Megan Rose (9)
St Catherine's Primary School, Belfast

Food, Glorious Food

Can I borrow a few pounds?
Why?
'Cause I'm broke.
Why?
Where's my belt?
Why?
I'm not telling you.
Why?
Where is it when you need it?
Why?
Actually I want my knife and fork.
Why?
You look tasty.
Why?
Mmmmmmmmmm!
Why? . . . argh!
(licking lips)
That was a feast.
W . . . ?

Michaela Mulholland (9)
St Catherine's Primary School, Belfast

Lonely Sitting Here

I am lonely sitting here by myself
And no one here
It's quiet
It is dull
I'm by myself with no fun
I am sad because there is
No one to talk to.

Sammy-Jo Madden (10)
St Catherine's Primary School, Belfast

Why, Why, Why?

I'm just going shopping, I'll be back in a minute.
Why?
To get some messages.
Why?
Because we need some food.
Why?
Because we will be hungry.
Why?
Because it gives us energy.
Why?
Because we can grow.
Why?
Because we need healthy food to grow.
Why?
Why don't you stop saying that boring word 'why'
Why?
That's why!

Rachel Annesley (9)
St Catherine's Primary School, Belfast

I Didn't Hand My Homework In Because . . .

I didn't hand my homework in because
My mum put it in the post!

I didn't hand my homework in because
My dog ate it!

I didn't hand my homework in because
My pencil was in a terrible mood!

I didn't hand my homework in because
My rubber rubbed it all out when I wasn't looking!

I didn't hand my homework in because
I did do it *but* I just forgot to write it down!

Patricia Savage (9)
St Catherine's Primary School, Belfast

Down Town

I'm going down town.
Why?
To buy new clothes.
Why?
Because you ate all of mine.
Why?
You said you were feeling peckish.
Why?
Ehhh, shut up.
Why?
Did I mention I was a cannibal.
Why? Why are you eating me?
Because you're young and full of blood.
Why?

Sarah Graham (9)
St Catherine's Primary School, Belfast

Why?

Your cousins are coming over.
Why?
To play.
Why?
Because it is sunny.
Why?
The sun is shining.
Why?
Because that what it does.
Why?
Why don't you stop saying 'Why'?
Why?

Eileen Donnelly (8)
St Catherine's Primary School, Belfast

Forever Friends

I thought I had a friend (forever too I thought).
It turns out I don't have one at all.

I need another friend to comfort me
And stay my friend for life.

Be my friend, oh please, be my one. Oh yeah!

I've found a friend, a friend I can trust.
That friend I've found.
To be my only friend I need.

Margaret-Rose Tully (10)
St Catherine's Primary School, Belfast

The Wonderful World of Candy!

Would you like to live and grow
In a land all full of snow
Where doors and walls are chocolate-brown,
And candy canes, there are no frowns.
Where happy faces always smile,
And some sick children for a while
The place that no one buys the sweets
You just eat, eat, eat, and *eat!*

Kelly-Anne McCullough (10)
St Catherine's Primary School, Belfast

Imagine That

Imagine you could jump and dance
In a playground made of plants!
Would you swing or take a ride
On a leaf or a petal slide?

Gemma Kearney (9)
St Catherine's Primary School, Belfast

Property

Once at a moment
round the bend
stood a scary
little shed.
Flames of fire
on top of roofs
cats and ghosts
opening doors
smelly old rats,
lying on floors.

Mary-Louise Bunting (10)
St Catherine's Primary School, Belfast

I Hate Poems

I hate poems really bad
When we have to study them
It makes me very sad.
Lots of words and lots of rhymes
I hate poems all the time.
Words and words that keep on going
I would rather do some sewing.

Siobhan Cunningham (10)
St Catherine's Primary School, Belfast

A Best Friend

A best friend is a rose that never dies
A best friend is a leaf on a tree that never falls
A best friend never lies
A best friend runs like a gentle breeze
A best friend talks like a whisper
You should have a best friend like mine!

Kirsten Brannigan (10)
St Catherine's Primary School, Belfast

My Dog

I have a dog called Kim
Who likes to sit on the bin
She loves to swim.

She chews on your shoes
And watches the news
When she has the blues.

She destroyed the table and the chairs
Then jumped up and stole the pears
And headed off for the stairs.

Nicola Moyes (11)
St Catherine's Primary School, Belfast

Friends

I'm going out with my friends.
Why?
Because my friends want me to.
Why?
Because I am going out to shop with my friends.
Why?
Because I want to.
Why?
Will you stop asking me 'Why?'
Why?

Niamh Flynn (9)
St Catherine's Primary School, Belfast

One Strange Morning

This morning I buttered my bread
The knife turned round and buttered me instead.
The cat jumped on my head
I think I'll go back to bed!

Hannah Murray (10)
St Catherine's Primary School, Belfast

Animals

There are a lot of different animals
Around this big wide world
Some are stripy and spotty
Some are large and small
Some have big long necks
Some have floppy ears
Some have small, circular tails
Some have sharp white teeth
Some animals can jump
Some can hide in their shells
But the best thing about animals
Is that you can keep them as your pets.

Stacey Quinn (10)
St Catherine's Primary School, Belfast

Why?

What are you doing?
Why?
I'm doing my homework.
Why?
Because if I don't I will get shouted at.
Why?
Because I have to learn.
Why?
Why don't you zip your mouth for once!
Why?
Oh do shut up for once and stop staying 'Why!'
OK, but why?

Emma Magee (8)
St Catherine's Primary School, Belfast

What Is Brown?

Brown is for a violin.
Brown is often for people's eyes.
Brown is for muck on a field.
Brown is often on someone's T shirt.
Brown is people's hair.
Brown is a colour of bricks.
Brown is a colour of our school's desks.
Brown is a darkish colour.
Brown is a paint colour.
Brown is a crayon colour.
Brown sometimes can be a birthday present.
Brown is the colour of a chair.
Brown is my best colour.
Brown could be your favourite colour.
Brown is the best colour ever.

Pearse Conor Mooney (8)
St Gall's Primary School, Belfast

What Is Gold?

Gold is what makes me sing.
Gold is paint.
Gold is heavy.
Gold is strong.
Gold as a gong.
Gold is God.
Gold is Heaven.
Gold is God's light.
Gold is wonderful.

Patrick Kilifin (8)
St Gall's Primary School, Belfast

What Is Black?

Black is my hair colour
Black is a dark sky
Black is the colour of our cat
Black is the colour of tarmac
Black is the colour of an eyelash
Black is the colour of my pen
Black is the colour of a crow
Black is the colour of my dog
Black is the colour of my coat
Black is the colour of coal.
Black is a colour.

Donn Whelan (8)
St Gall's Primary School, Belfast

My Medicine

A snake on top of a cake.
Cats' claws and dirty jaws.
Then a big whack of ham and jam on top.
Then a snail who has a dirty nail.
Then a dead head laying on a dirty bed
and there you have it,
George's marvellous medicine!

Gary Marron (8)
St Gall's Primary School, Belfast

What Is Gold?

Gold is shiny.
Gold is treasure.
Gold is strong.
Gold is special.
Gold is the sunshine.
Gold is a lion.

Matthew Walker (8)
St Gall's Primary School, Belfast

What Is Silver?

Silver is a car.
Silver is a shiny colour.
Silver is a nice colour.
Silver is a star.
Silver is a coat.
Silver is a sparkling colour.
Silver is a spaceship.
Silver is a silvery colour.
Silver is a beautiful silvery colour.
Silver is a wonderful also a shiny colour.

Nathan Maginn (7)
St Gall's Primary School, Belfast

What Is Yellow?

Yellow is the sun.
Yellow is a giraffe.
Yellow is sand.
Yellow is a day on the beach.
Yellow is just like gold.
Yellow is a book cover.
Yellow is a light.
Yellow is Lego.
Yellow is plastic.

Daniel Donnan (8)
St Gall's Primary School, Belfast

My Magic Poem

A magic medicine it shall be
Strong cold tea and salt from the sea.
Give me a bug or crocodile three
Give me a bug or snail or two.
A sweet from the ground or a fly or two.
Give me a fish's fin and a stinky, off banana
Two spoonfuls of loads of raw ham.
Half of a tree and a sticky knee.
Granny dear, look what I have here!
Hope you'll like it,
You'll go bonkers, I hear!

Ryan Casson (8)
St Gall's Primary School, Belfast

My Magic Medicine

My magic medicine for grandma is
a snake on top of a cake.
A dead head on a smelly bed
and a nail of a snail.
A piece of ham inside a frying pan.
A pair of claws with ugly jaws
and a giant pig with an earwig.
Will she be dead? Will she have no head?
Will it make her be sick or make her thick?

James Brennan (8)
St Gall's Primary School, Belfast

Red Is . . .

Red is my favourite colour
Red is a sign for bad
Red is a colour
Red is a rose
Red are our valentine's cards
Red are our books
Red is Christmas
Red are lips.

Michael Meehan (7)
St Gall's Primary School, Belfast

My Medicine Poem

Hubble bubble there is trouble
Peas from the seas, salt and fault.
A big fat head and two loaves of bread
A big whack of ham and a spoonful of jam
She'll be blind, oh so kind!
Six carts and two darts
One happiness bite and one bottle of fright.
This will do the trick and make her flick.

Niall Carson (8)
St Gall's Primary School, Belfast

My Medicine Poem

Dirty jeans and smelly old beans
And a big whack of ham and a spoonful of jam
So do not be mean, but be a bean
And if you are blind you will be very kind.
So if I make the bar pink you cannot get a drink.
So get ready because rub-a-dub-dub
My medicine is in a tub.
So get ready for this, my granny!

Ciaran Donnelly (9)
St Gall's Primary School, Belfast

My Medicine

A magic medicine it shall be.
Strong cold tea and salt from the sea.
Some dogs' paws and crocodiles' jaws.
Five rats and six bats.
Get a sleeping twit, chuck him in a pit.
A toad that will knock her flying down the road.
Ripped jeans and some cold baked beans.
Six slugs and two rugs.
I'll stir them up, I'll boil them long
A mixture tough, a mixture strong
I don't care for so long
If it's right or if it's wrong!

Conor Malone (8)
St Gall's Primary School, Belfast

My Magic Medicine

So give me a bug and a lizard three,
Give me two snails and a jumping flea,
I need a shark from the sea.
I'll stir them up and boil them long,
I'll make sure the mixture's strong.
And then high-ho and down it goes,
A good big spoonful (hold your nose).
Just gulp it down and have no fear
Oh, Granny, if you knew
What I have got in store for you!

Fiontain Kennedy (9)
St Gall's Primary School, Belfast

Stephen's Marvellous Medicine

Give me a bug and a snail or two
Two spoons full of jam with loads of raw ham
A rat from the sewers and a jug of dirty water.
A bar of soap, she definitely won't cope.
So give me a bumblebee, a lizard, maybe three
Cats' food, dogs' droppings, half a tree and a bit of a knee.
A fish's fin, everything that came straight from the bin
Crunchy autumn leaves and her very own rotten toenails.
Will she melt?
Will she explode?
Who knows she might even turn into a toad!

Stephen Maginn (9)
St Gall's Primary School, Belfast

Colours

Blue is very colourful.
Blue is my second best colour.
Blue is the colour of glass.
Blue is the colour of the sky.
Blue is a crayon.
Blue is a colour of Lego.
Bull is the colour of my science book.
Blue is the colour of my history book.
Blue is the colour of Leinster.

Aaron Slane (7)
St Gall's Primary School, Belfast

Chef

A chef is white
Like winter snow
In the kitchen
He is warm
A chef's hat
Like a cooker
He's 'Ready Steady Cook'.

Eamonn Quinn (10)
St John The Baptist Boys' Primary School, Belfast

Evil

Evil is horrible
It feels very scary
It sounds very loud
And it looks very hairy
It smells like rotten eggs
And tastes like garlic
Its colour is dark green
And I hate its fat body.

Colm Molloy (11)
St John The Baptist Boys' Primary School, Belfast

Fireman

A fireman is red
He is the summer
In a fire station
He is bright and sunny
A fireman is a fireproof suit
A long metal pole
He would be on TV sometimes
A burnt bit of toast.

Ryan Bowman (11)
St John The Baptist Boys' Primary School, Belfast

Smelly Digestive System

My foot gets chewed and chewed,
Then it is very rude,
Next it gets ground
And my teeth can't even find it.

Then sometimes I spit,
It even gets lit,
It is so wet,
It is like a smelly armpit.

My food then travels,
I feel like gravel,
It feels so weird,
It is like I have a beard.

My food gets turned into gas,
That's why I need a mask,
My food goes to my bum,
Now it is so round like a plum.

Conor Donnelly (9)
St John The Baptist Boys' Primary School, Belfast

Wacky Blood

My blood is pumped round my body
like mud rolling down a hill.
My cells travel like gravel
being led out on a road.
My heart pumps as fast
as a kart going down a hill.
My blood speeds past my spine
like a mine going off in a car.
The heart pumps lumps of blood around my body
like ramps on a busy road.

Michael Duffin (9)
St John The Baptist Boys' Primary School, Belfast

Crazy Digestion

The food goes into the grinding of my teeth,
It goes into the grinding of tiny shreds,
All it does is feel the grief,
The carbohydrate called the bread.

It follows down to the liver,
Which it mixes with an acid,
Then flows in the blood like a river,
Which takes it to another organ.

The food is now in the small intestine,
All to take the good food out,
The roughage and water goes to the large intestine,
For it to travel all about.

All the large intestine's waste,
Travels all the way to the bladder,
It all comes out like a paste,
Down a tube like a ladder.

Conor McGrath (9)
St John The Baptist Boys' Primary School, Belfast

Strange Digestive

My teeth are grinding.
While they're grinding
My food is getting a lot of grief.
It travels mostly unravelling
All the way down the gullet.

It gets pushed by the muscle
Always having a hustle.
It unravels to the stomach.

It goes into the intestine
Makes the suggestion,
Should it go to the blood
Or go to waste?

Conal Sheppard (9)
St John The Baptist Boys' Primary School, Belfast

Springtime

Frogs hopping everywhere
New tadpoles being born.
Birds flying over the land
Singing happily round the land.
Plants getting more colourful
And farmers growing their crops.

I hear farmers going in tracks
I'm hearing their beepers.
Longer days for them
Harder days for them.
Hotter and hotter days for them.
Farmers working harder and harder.

I hear a newborn lamb being born.
Crying and baaing to its mother.
I hear it stop because it smiles.
The sweet, sweet grass and sweet flowers.

Ryan Hegarty (9)
St John The Baptist Boys' Primary School, Belfast

Slimy, Slippery Blood

First the slimy blood is travelling up to the heart,
Like the sticky mud is unravelling from a cart.

Then the muscles push the blood up to the lung,
Which kind of makes me want to hum.

The blood carries proteins and all that to all the places
Which need them and that's what Tommy's mummy's
Been trying to feed him.

Louis Donnelly (9)
St John The Baptist Boys' Primary School, Belfast

Season Spring

In the fields tractors starting
Because the seeds need sowing
The rumbling, the grinding
The ground needs fertilising.

Longer days, no more short
Getting bright with more sun
The sun is shining like a big bright bun
And little patches of cloud

No more cold, it's getting warmer
A new horizon with a higher temperature
No more snow, just warmth and fun
I'll hate it when spring is all done

Look in the sky the birds are returning
Flying in the sky they are singing
Singing happily while they're flying
Now all the worms are going to be eaten.

Now it is time for the festivals
Easter with the egg hunt and chocolate
St Patrick's Day is when everybody dresses in green
Shamrocks, fun and lots of ice cream.

Frog spawn is opening and tadpoles are coming out
It is new birth for them, they have to grow
They have to go through a big long cycle
They're going to develop lungs and a loud ribbit.

In spring I climb my granny's tree
I am a good fast climber, just like a monkey
Games in the street, everybody is running
When someone scores the air is filled with cheering.

Plants are coming out, bees and wasps too
Feeding on the plants' nectar, flies too
Air is filled with buzzing
While all the other insects are sucking.

Look around, everything is green
And the sky is blue too
It's green instead of grey
While the sun is the colour of hay.

There is baaing everywhere in the fields
Newborn lambs hide behind mothers like shields
The sun is setting over the new horizon
Looks like spring is the loveliest season.

Gareth May (10)
St John The Baptist Boys' Primary School, Belfast

Life In Spring

In spring I can hear lambs cry
As they walk in fields and pass by
Where tractors would cut grass
So it turns to the colour of bass
Out in streets people would play
Where they would have fun and scream all day
I would say to myself, 'I love spring'
To see blossoms bloom and swallows sing.

In lakes I would see green frogs
And the young tadpoles jump on logs
I would feel the sun against me
And I would be happy and feel so free
Birds return to their nest
And I think the biggest are the best
Sometimes I would go fishing
When I catch one it flaps its wing.

In Easter my family come to my house
Where they would make a lot of noise
They would come just to have fun
To celebrate what history has done
That is spring and it's a beautiful season
And you know it's there for a reason
To enjoy and have fun
And also enjoy the sun.

Gary Crossan (10)
St John The Baptist Boys' Primary School, Belfast

Colours

White is for snow
It can bite off your toe

Blue is for the sky
It's in my school tie

Green man is the code for 'cross'
And also for moss

Red is for Mars all covered in dust
A holiday there has to be 'a must'!

Yellow is for light
All glaring and bright

Black is for night
And being tucked up tight

Follow the rainbow - right to the end
Follow the arch right around the bend
That's where we're told
We'll find a pot of gold!

Jonathan Morrissey (11)
St John The Baptist Boys' Primary School, Belfast

Green, Black

Black
Black is the colour of the sky at night.
Black is the colour that gives you a fright.
Black is the colour that scares you at night.
Black is the colour for me.

Green
Green like a cucumber that grows in the grass.
Green like the apple that lives in the tree.
Green leaves rot when winter winds blow.
Green is the best.

Gerard O'Rawe (10)
St John The Baptist Boys' Primary School, Belfast

Yellow

Yellow is for the shiny sun,
Yellow for the icing on my bun,
Yellow is for the autumn leaves,
Yellow is for the black and yellow on the bees,
Yellow is for very dirty teeth,
Yellow is for lemons and the bitterness beneath,
Yellow is for the egg yolk,
Yellow is for the sponge we soak,
Yellow is the best,
So many rhyming words than all the rest.

Peter Forde (11)
St John The Baptist Boys' Primary School, Belfast

Come Now Thy Winter

Few are the birds and animals in winter
Robin's birdbath is no more
Over all the dense cold air at dawn
Sighs from people getting up in the morn
The winter's here and I do believe
It's here to stay.

Kurtis McGreevy (11)
St John The Baptist Boys' Primary School, Belfast

Red

Red is the colour when I cut my nose,
Red is the colour of the petals on a rose,
Red is my face when I'm in a rush,
Red is my face when I begin to blush,
Red is the colour of the sunset in the sky,
Red is the colour of a cherry pie.

Michael Adair (11)
St John The Baptist Boys' Primary School, Belfast

Men Of Mars

One night as I went to bed,
I saw a strange object in the sky,
I went to sleep and dreamed about
Little green men and UFOs,
I woke up then and it came true,
I was in an alien spacecraft,
In my bed all snug and warm,
I thought I must have been dreaming,
Because surely this couldn't happen,
A little green man in a spacesuit
Came up to me and said,
'We want to test and scan you,
And this thing you call a bed.'
This little man was weird,
Strange in every way,
He had a thin, bony body
And a rather large head.
I stared in amazement,
As that little green man,
Called to ten other little green men,
To come and lift me and carry me out,
'Yahoo!' I shouted out,
'I'll be the first ever person to set foot on Mars!'

Eoghan Murray (10)
St John The Baptist Boys' Primary School, Belfast

Green Nature

Green is for grass
Green is for trees
Green is the grass on my dirty knees
Green is for the hills, which swallow the sun
Green is for everything that is fun.

Emmet McPoland (11)
St John The Baptist Boys' Primary School, Belfast

Black

Black is the colour of black ice
Black is the colour of dying-looking mice
Black is what all Goths wear
Black is the colour of numbers on a dice
Black is the colour I think isn't nice.

Karl Dowdall (10)
St John The Baptist Boys' Primary School, Belfast

The Way I See Black

At night when the sky is black
That's when I hit the sack
But when the sky is blue again
I go back to school, which drives me insane
Then at breaktime if someone hits me I see black
This only happens when there's a great impact
Then lunchtime comes and the sausages are black
The food is horrible that's a fact
Then after the day in the street I get whacked
So that's how sometimes you see black
And that's my friend's craic.

Darren Cosgrove (11)
St John The Baptist Boys' Primary School, Belfast

Love Everyone

L ove my mum on Saturday,
O pen the door for my mum
V alentine's Day, send me a card,
E very day be good for your teacher.

Damien Barton (9)
St John The Baptist Boys' Primary School, Belfast

Pink Perfect

Pink is a dream of people's hearts.
It thinks about the kindness of love.
It remembers the clouds up above.
It forgets the stars.
It tells us the world is full of peace.

Alanna Flynn (8)
St Mark's Primary School, Dunmurry

Red

Red dreams of love
It thinks of life
It remembers God's creation
Red forgets all the bad things in life
Red tells us to be good.

Caitlin Duffy (8)
St Mark's Primary School, Dunmurry

Blue

Blue dreams about waves crashing.
Its thoughts are about the big blue sky.
It remembers a rainbow.
Blue forgets all the bad things in the world.
Blue tells us that it's raining.

Gary Campbell Smyth (9)
St Mark's Primary School, Dunmurry

Blue

Blue is the colour of the sky.
It is the colour of my dreams at night.
It thinks of a war, is it going to stop?

Nadeen Whelan (8)
St Mark's Primary School, Dunmurry

Red

It dreams of love.
It thinks of God's blood.
It remembers fun and friendship.
It forgets hatred.
It tells us to be respectful.

Thomas Hughes (9)
St Mark's Primary School, Dunmurry

Red

Red dreams of blood.
Red has thoughts of love.
Red remembers Jesus' kindness.
Red forgets badness.
Red tells us what to do and what not to do.

Anthony Rooney (9)
St Mark's Primary School, Dunmurry

Red

Red makes a heart
It says, 'Don't be bad.'
Red makes a fire
Red is love.

Dominic O'Prey (9)
St Mark's Primary School, Dunmurry

Orange

Orange dreams of the sun.
It thinks of the rainbow in the sky.
I remember the colour of leaves.
Orange forgets all the bad things.

Thomas Kerr (8)
St Mark's Primary School, Dunmurry

Child

Child of the past
Sleeping on straw, so ragged and dirty

Child of the present
Sleeping in beds, so soft and comfortable

Child of the past
So hungry and thirsty, they search the streets

Child of the present
I'm stuffed and fed, what more can I eat?

Child of the past
During the day they search and sell

Child of the present
On PlayStation, Splinter Cell

Child of the past
They work in school and play skipping games

Child of the present
I read and write and jump about

Child of the past
They feel so lonely and sad

Child of the present
I feel so thoughtful and kind.

Joshua Galway (11)
St Mark's Primary School, Dunmurry

Blue Is My Favourite Colour

Blue dreams of God
It has thoughts of stars and sky.
It forgets hate and sadness.
It tells us it's our friend.
It tells us it would never run away from being a friend.

Claire Begley (9)
St Mark's Primary School, Dunmurry

Child

Child of the past
All cold and lonely

Child of the present
All warm and comfy

Child of the past
All tired and weary

Child of the present
In bed all warm

Child of the past
All starved and hungry

Child of the present
Eating food, yum yummy

Child of the past
Selling things on cold streets

Child of the present
Sitting in the classroom heat

Child of the past
Skipping ropes, that's all

Child of the present
Board games, PlayStation and ball.

Kelly Duffy (11)
St Mark's Primary School, Dunmurry

Wind

Wind whistling through the city
Wind blowing under the trees
Blow, blow, blow
Wind rumbling beside the waterfall
Wind give me your breath.

Hannah Denvir (9)
St Mark's Primary School, Dunmurry

Volcano Nathan

My head is made of footballs
My bones are made of trees
My hair is made of cauliflower
And my belly is full of bees.

My hands are made of tulips
My eyes are made of stars
My blood is made of lava
My ears come from Mars.

My thoughts are cross-eyed bats
My dreams are sitting cats
I'm all mixed up as you can see
And all that's here I'm glad to be.

Nathan McGonnell (9)
St Mark's Primary School, Dunmurry

Blue

Blue always dreams of Mary,
Blue always thinks of sea and peace,
Blue remembers saints and the dead,
Blue forgets all bad things,
Blue tells us what to do.

Eoin Curley (9)
St Mark's Primary School, Dunmurry

Gold

Gold dreams of gold rings.
Gold thinks of the sun.
Gold remembers Heaven's gates opening.
Gold forgets leaves falling on the ground.
Gold tells us it is happy.

Christina Magennis (9)
St Mark's Primary School, Dunmurry

Sun, Sun

Sun, sun everywhere,
Sun, sun in the air.
Sun, sun blazing like a gun,
Sun, sun let's have some fun.
Sun, sun shines so bright,
Sun, sun goes down at night.

Shauna Briggs (10)
St Mark's Primary School, Dunmurry

The Blues

When I lose my favourite shoes
That's the blues
When my sister gets more than me
That's the blues
When I get ignored
That's the blues.

Georgia Perry (9)
St Mark's Primary School, Dunmurry

Red

Red dreams of Man U
Red thinks of Arsenal losing
Red remembers Scholes scoring a goal
Red forgets Beckham because he moved
Red tells us that Man U are the champions.

Andrew Kettle (8)
St Mark's Primary School, Dunmurry

Colours

If I were red
I'd be a rose
Growing in a meadow.

If I were blue
I'd be a river
Flowing gently to the sea.

If I were green
I'd be grass
Dozing in the countryside.

If I were brown
I'd be a tree
Drawing life
Up from the soil.

If I were silver
I'd be a firefly
Flickering in the dark.

If I were gold,
I'd be the sun
Blazing free.

Courtney Thomas (8)
St Mark's Primary School, Dunmurry

Red

Red dreams of love
It has thoughts of being cared for.

Red forgets to do things
Red remembers to love others
Red tells us to be kind.

Niamh Hamill (9)
St Mark's Primary School, Dunmurry

Purple

Purple dreams of love throughout the world.
Purple thinks of beautiful flowers.
Purple remembers peace.
Purple forgets fighting.
Purple tells us to be kind.

Gabriella Norney (9)
St Mark's Primary School, Dunmurry

Blue

Blue dreams of the sea in its vision
Blue thinks of the sun in the sky
Blue remembers the death of Christ
Blue forgets all the bad things in life
And blue tells us to stay outside.

Leia Corr (9)
St Mark's Primary School, Dunmurry

Red

Red dreams of happiness
Its thoughts are everlasting life
Red remembers sadness
It forgets blood
It tells us about glory.

Conor Moylan (8)
St Mark's Primary School, Dunmurry

Sun

Sun, sun shining so bright
All through the morning light.
All day and all night
Shining so bright is the moon at night.

Tanya McCarry (10)
St Mark's Primary School, Dunmurry

Jumbled Up James

My arms are made of brown trees
My feet are made of bouncy balls
My hands are made of floppy ham
My chest is made of cold waterfalls

My legs are made of planks of wood
My neck is made of black pot
My fingers are made of fat pencils
There's no wonder I've lost the plot!

My nose is made of Swiss cheese
My ears are made of high cliffs
My mouth is made of a wet sewer
I just went all stiff!

My thoughts are made of blank zebras
My dreams are made of sleeping bags
I'm all mixed up as you can see
And all that's here I'm glad to be.

James McDermott (9)
St Mark's Primary School, Dunmurry

Don't Match

Pets and football just don't match,
My dog can't score, his name is Patch.

He can't score from the halfway line,
Why does this dog have to be mine?

Cats just can't score a goal,
Nor can an otter, monkey or mole.

Some pets can score anywhere on the pitch,
I'm gonna ask Lilo to give me Stitch!

Stitch can score from Brazil to here,
My dog can't score a centimetre near.

Mark Ormerod (10)
St Mark's Primary School, Dunmurry

The Dodger

There's this wee man from Ireland,
He plays for a team called Kilkenny,
He gets called 'The Dodger',
'Cause he's as fast as a cheetah,
People are saying he's the best,
He never stops scoring,
'Cause he never has that hurl out of his hand.
His name is DJ Cairey,
The champion of hurling
Everyone loves him and so do I,
He'll always be my hero.

Thomas Manning (10)
St Mark's Primary School, Dunmurry

Where In The World?

Where in the world do you think I'd be?
Take my hand, come and see.
Sometimes I'd be in Africa
To see the lions and giraffes
Or sometimes I would go to England
To see the Queen and her palace.
Then I would go to Rome,
Meet the Pope then go home,
But most times I like to be alone
With my family in our little dome.

Lauren McMahon (10)
St Mark's Primary School, Dunmurry

My Cousin's Feet

My cousin's feet are smelly,
He has very smelly feet.
They smell like egg and onion
But his feet I would not eat.

Gerard McAreavey (10)
St Mark's Primary School, Dunmurry

Weather

What is the sun?
A huge, golden, sparkling, dazzling ball in the sky.
What is the rain?
Rain is God's tears dripping from Heaven.
Where does snow come from?
Snow comes from the feathers of the angels' wings
Falling down from Heaven.
Who sends the wind?
Birds flapping their wings.
What is my favourite weather?
Sunny, because you can have water fights,
Have fun and get a tan.

Djamila Boudissa (11)
St Mark's Primary School, Dunmurry

Ashes To Ashes

Everyone agrees that my dad's a great bloke
But I just don't understand why he likes to suck in smoke.

It's dirty and it's smelly, I think you all agree
That when someone smokes they're just like a chimney.

I mean, what is so good about smoking a cancer stick?
It turns your lungs black and makes you very sick.

But really all it does, from your toes to your eyelashes
Is kill you stone dead and turn you from ashes to ashes.

Mark Walsh (11)
St Mark's Primary School, Dunmurry

My Home

H is for the warm home that I live in
O is for others who live with me
M is for my mum who looks after me
E is for everyone, happy in their home.

Ashton McLaughlin (10)
St Mark's Primary School, Dunmurry

There Was An Old Woman

There was an old woman who could fly,
Nobody knows quite why,
Maybe she got her powers,
By talking to flowers,
That old woman who could fly.

There was an old woman in Peru,
She got stuck to her wall with glue,
She was stuck there for days,
Until she finally got away,
From that sticky wall in Peru.

There was an old woman who loved pies,
If she didn't get any, she cried,
She ate a pie every day,
Until she finally blew away,
That old woman who loved pies.

There was an old woman who laid eggs,
She had very, very long legs,
She was just like a hen;
She stayed in a pen,
That old woman who laid eggs.

There was an old woman who loved to drive,
She was having the time of her life,
Until she knocked down a boy,
And broke all his toys,
She's lucky she's alive!

Noel Bradley-Johnston (10)
St Mark's Primary School, Dunmurry

The Home Poem

H is for the house I live in
O is for the others who live there
M is for my family
E is for everyone is happy.

Louise McClenaghan (11)
St Mark's Primary School, Dunmurry

Sam

Sam running swiftly
falling one, two, three.
Where he goes no one knows,
it's a mystery.
So running swiftly, angrily
is a bad idea if you ask me.
Poor old Sam
shouldn't have been acting like a ram,
or he wouldn't have hit that tree.

Corey Hamill (10)
St Mark's Primary School, Dunmurry

Lunch Of The Week

Monday's lunch is tuna sandwiches,
Tuesday's lunch is wrapped in bandages,
Wednesday's lunch is very boring,
Thursday's lunch has my friend snoring,
Friday's lunch is Shredded Wheat,
Saturday's lunch was going tweet, tweet, tweet,
Sunday's lunch was the best of all
But then it ended up on the wall.

Emma Brown (11)
St Mark's Primary School, Dunmurry

Stars

Stars, stars everywhere
Stars, stars here and there
Stars, stars shining bright
Stars, stars out at night
Stars, stars like a light
Stars, stars what a delight.

Patrick Hope (11)
St Mark's Primary School, Dunmurry

The Adventure

Going here, going there
Oh my God! Is that a bear?
Running away fast, fast, fast
Then the bear stops at last.

I slowed down, huffing and puffing,
The bear returned to the woods.
I ran home to my mum and dad
And told them about the adventure I had.

Michael McConnell (10)
St Mark's Primary School, Dunmurry

Haunted House

One fine summer's day
My friend and I went out to play
Outside that freaky house

The place was dark and grey
I was just about to say
Before the ghost scared us away
From outside that freaky house.

Zachary Gordon (10)
St Mark's Primary School, Dunmurry

The Joke

'My house is on fire,' said Mrs Liar.
'Who said that?' asked Mr Bat.
'It came from over there,' said Mr Meer.
'Let's go over,' said Mrs Rover.
'Call nine, nine, nine,' said Mr Vine.
'Stop, it's a joke!' said Mr Poke.
'She tricked all of us,' said Mrs Fuss.

Gavin McKee (11)
St Mark's Primary School, Dunmurry

Colours

If I were red I'd be a berry
Growing on a Christmas bush.

If I were blue I'd be a bluebell
Ringing in the woods.

If I were white
I'd be a snowflake.

If I were purple
I'd be the night sky
Covering the world.

James Maguire (9)
St Mark's Primary School, Dunmurry

Ghost Of The Week

Monday's ghost is full of toast,
Tuesday's ghost is full of roast,
Wednesday's ghost will fall apart,
Thursday's ghost will never part,
Friday's ghost is really keen,
Saturday's ghost is truly mean,
Sunday's ghost goes . . . *boo!*

Devina Whelan (11)
St Mark's Primary School, Dunmurry

Pretty Pets Alliteration

P retty proud pampered puppies
E xcellent excited extra elephants
T houghtful thrilling tidy tigers
S lidy shrilling shiny snakes.

Brendan McStravick (10)
St Mark's Primary School, Dunmurry

Colours

If I were white, I'd be a feather
Drifting slowly through the air.

If I were scarlet
I'd be a forest fox's brush.

If I were azure
I'd be the brightest sky ever.

If I were silver
I'd be a bird flying overhead.

If I were golden
I'd be a leaf-swathed path in autumn.

If I were green
I'd be an oxygen giving plant.

Michelle Russell (9)
St Mark's Primary School, Dunmurry

Colours

If I were yellow
I'd be the setting sun.

If I were blue
I'd be a dolphin
diving in the deep.

If I were white
I'd be a snowdrop
sleeping in
the wintry snow.

If I were green
I'd be a leafy wood.

Kirsty Mulligan (9)
St Mark's Primary School, Dunmurry

The Mixed Up Body

My ears are made of root beer
My nose is made of holey cheese
My arms are made of long leaves
My toes are made of stinging bees.

My chest is made of greasy peas
My cheeks are made of sticky flies
My eyes are made of apple pies
Could you eat me please?

My legs are made of hard stones
My fingers are made of rotten bones
My heart is made of green plums
My hands are made of grey milk.

My thoughts are of no school days
My dreams are scary and mad
My wishes are no school ways
My feelings are hurt so bad.

I'm all mixed up as you can see
And all that's here I'm glad to be.

Christopher Keenan (9)
St Mark's Primary School, Dunmurry

My Horrible Big Sister

My horrible big sister,
All she does is shout,
She makes me do her laundry
And hang her knickers out!

She never takes me anywhere
And she makes me do lots and lots,
But the worst thing she makes me do
Is take off her smelly socks!

Natasha McCann (10)
St Mark's Primary School, Dunmurry

Winter

The sound of the carol singing, 'Jingle Bells, Jingle Bells'
The sound of the snapping cracker, crack, crack
The taste of the Christmas dinner, yum, yum
The taste of the chocolate running in my mouth
The sight of the people laughing, 'Ha, ha'
The sight of the decorations shining in my eyes
The touch of the warm fire going up my hands
The touch of the wrapping paper, crunch, crunch
The smell of the candy canes in my hands
The smell of the Christmas tree.

Stephanie Brown (10)
St Mark's Primary School, Dunmurry

Grannies

Grannies are helpful and mental
Grannies are mad and bad
Grannies are fun, they love the sun
Grannies are glum without the sun.

Grannies have friends that bend
Grannies walk and talk
Grannies can bark and sark
Grannies are punky and funky.

Ashleigh McManus (10)
St Mark's Primary School, Dunmurry

Singing Birds

Birds fly through the sky
Birds peck near the ground
Birds walk along the grass
Birds dance beyond the flowers.

Matthew Cassidy (8)
St Mark's Primary School, Dunmurry

Mixed Up Niamh

My legs are made of bony rocks
My chest is made of smelly old ham
My feet are made of very old trees
My arms are made of waterfalls.

My hair is made of Tigger's fur
My toes are made of Care Bears
My fingers are made of wallpaper
My lips are made of Tigger's nose.

My dreams are made of singing lips
My thoughts are made of dancing cats
My wishes are made of talking dogs
My feelings are made of pink bears.

I'm all mixed up as you can see
And all that's here I'm glad to be.

Care Bear Niamh.

Niamh Kelly (9)
St Mark's Primary School, Dunmurry

Why Am I So Delicious?

My arms are made of water snake
My fingers are made of ten pencils

My heart is made of squeezed love
My ears are made of twirled stencils

My feet are made of wiggly worms
My eyes are made of everlasting gobstoppers

My hair is made of cold spaghetti
My thoughts are made of everyone's needs

I'm all mixed up as you can see
And all that's here I'm glad to be.

Mary Rose Duffy (9)
St Mark's Primary School, Dunmurry

My Pup

I have a dog as white as snow
And in the dark she makes a glow

When I'm cold
She cuddles me up,
That is why she's my favourite pup

She's the best in the west,
She's called Jess,
She will bark in the dark,
But she knows not to tickle

I love her hair
And I love her,
That is why I really care.

Rebecca May (10)
St Mark's Primary School, Dunmurry

Colours

If I were silver
I'd be a river flowing
Through the countryside.

If I were gold
I'd be a star
Gleaming up on high.

If I were turquoise
I'd be the sea
Swishing past mountains.

Ruairi Carlile (8)
St Mark's Primary School, Dunmurry

My Gran

She is loveable but maybe not beautiful.
Well, what else do I have to say?
She's big, fat and hairy.
I hate to say it.
She looks like a boy.
She sings, she snores, she keeps you awake
But she is my gran so I love her.
What more can I say, oh okay I guess.
She jumps, she's as smelly as a skunk but I love her.
So please no more.
Fine.
But this is the last of them all.
She is none of that stuff.

James McShane (10)
St Mark's Primary School, Dunmurry

The World

I've never been on a holiday
But I'm going on one soon
The day that I am going
Is the 22nd of June.

I hope I will have fun
Lying in the sun
Everything I'll miss
I'll give people a kiss.

I hope I will have fun
But the most important thing
Is I'm with my family
Playing in the sun!

Shannon McKee (9)
St Mark's Primary School, Dunmurry

My Family

I have a wonderful family,
They are so good to me.
Sometimes when I'm lonely
They cuddle up to me.
When I'm very sad
They always say, 'Be glad.'
The thing I love about my family,
Is they are always there for me.
Soon my mummy is having a baby
And it will be so much fun.
It will want to dance, sing and laugh
And be playful with everyone.

Sinead McParland (10)
St Mark's Primary School, Dunmurry

Rules

Do not jump on Father's toolbox
Do not munch on rotten eggs
Do not nurse a panther's baby
Do not try to grow four legs
Do not walk in muddy puddles
Do not sleep on Mother's chair
Never run in front of Grandma
Do not try to eat fresh air.

Karen McClenaghan (9)
St Mark's Primary School, Dunmurry

The Little Monster Haiku

Cute light brown rabbits
All different sizes too
I have one called Star.

Deborah Kennedy (10)
St Mark's Primary School, Dunmurry

Child

Child of the past
Has no warmth or heating
Child of the present
Has warmth while he's eating

Child of the past
Has not got a bed
Child of the present
Has a comfortable pillow
And is resting his head

Child of the past
Feels sad and looks bony
Child of the present
Never feels lonely

Child of the past
Has to work for his money
Child of the present
Sits at home and eats
Toast and honey

Child of the past
Gets hit with a cane
Child of the present
Gets grounded and told
Not to do it again

Child of the past
Hasn't got an education
In school
Child of the present
Comes home and plays
Snooker or pool.

Mark Mahon (11)
St Mark's Primary School, Dunmurry

Child

Child of the past
No food or water to eat or drink
Child of the present
All filled and water flows into the sink

Child of the past
Where do you sleep? In alleys and streets!
Child of the present
With blankets and pillows, a good night's sleep

Child of the past
Clothes are ragged and dirty
Child of the present
Clothes are all new and fluffy

Child of the past
Scared and weary
Child of the present
Happy and glad

Child of the past
House is all falling down
Child of the present
House is beautiful and warm

Child of the past
Games are so boring, marbles and clowns
Child of the present
Games are fun, like snakes and ladders and skipping, that's fun

Child of the past
Has maths and English and nothing else to do
Child of the present
English, maths, science and lots more to do

Child of the past
Out selling food and flowers
Child of the present
Out buying cakes and lovely red roses.

Orlaith Molloy (11)
St Mark's Primary School, Dunmurry

Child

Child of the past
In streets so cold.
Child of the present
Warm blankets to fold.

Child of the past
Has scraps to eat.
Child of the present
Has crisps and Shredded Wheat.

Child of the past
Running on his bare feet.
Child of the present
With clothes so neat.

Child of the past
Selling during the night.
Child of the present
Playing with his kite.

Child of the past
Getting hit on the hand.
Child of the present
Joining the school band.

Child of the past
Playing races.
Child of the present
Playing funny faces.

Child of the past
Feeling gloomy and sad.
Child of the present
Feeling happy and glad.

Anthony Speers (11)
St Mark's Primary School, Dunmurry

Child

Child of the past
Sleeps outside the door on the ground
Child of the present
Sleeps in a bed snug and sound

Child of the past
Has only a slice of bread
Child of the present
Makes toast from bread

Child of the past
Lives in a dirty, old wooden slum
Child of the present
Lives in a new strong home

Child of the past
Works long hours, selling oranges and plums
Child of the present
Plays happily all day in the sun

Child of the past
Is as daft as a cookie
Child of the present
Is as smart as a bookie

Child of the past
Plays with a small ball
Child of the present
Has PlayStation, games and all

Child of the past
Is lonely and sad
Child of the present
Is happy and glad.

Timothy Bradley (11)
St Mark's Primary School, Dunmurry

Child

Child of the past
Wearing ragged old clothes,
Sleeping in rooms with a family
All crammed in one bed.

Child of the present
Wearing their neat clean pyjamas,
While on their fluffy white pillow
They rest their sleepy head.

Child of the past,
Working a long, hard day,
Cleaning sooty chimneys
To earn a penny.

Child of the present
Another normal day,
Working hard in school
And learning plenty.

Child of the past
Earning money all day,
For a little bite to eat.

Child of the present
Waiting patiently for dinner,
Potatoes and meat.

Child of the past
Entertaining the rich
And opening cab doors.

Child of the present
Playing hide and go seek
By their front doors.

Child of the past
Very weak and sad.

Child of the present
Very active and glad.

Child of the past
Working as mudlarks.

Child of the present
Playing in the parks.

Anthony Todd (11)
St Mark's Primary School, Dunmurry

Child

Child of the past
Six in a bed
Child of the present
Somewhere cosy and warm to lay his head

Child of the past
Has no money and is starving
Child of the present
Has much more than a farthing

Child of the past
Is ragged and poor
Child of the present
Has clothes by the score

Child of the past
Has to work and has no play
Child of the present
Can play in the park throughout the day

Child of the past
Doesn't go to school no way!
Child of the present
Goes to school every day

Child of the past
Is lonely and sad
Child of the present
Has a loving mum and dad.

Tommy Davidson (11)
St Mark's Primary School, Dunmurry

Child

Child of the past
Has a doorstep for his head
Child of the present
Has pillows, blankets and bed

Child of the past
Has no shoes for his feet
Child of the present
Has shoes and lots to eat

Child of the past
Has marbles to play with
Child of the present
Has football and chess

Child of the past
Sleeps with lots of boys
Child of the present
Sleeps with teddies and toys

Child of the past
Can't write and read
Child of the present
Gets all he needs

Child of the past
Is weary and weak
Child of the present
Plays hide-and-seek

Child of the past
Has no father or mother
Child of the present
Has father, mother, sister and brother.

Daniel Maloney (11)
St Mark's Primary School, Dunmurry

Child

Child of the past
Lives on the street
Child of the present
Has a lot to eat

Child of the past
Entertains to be funny
Child of the present
Has a lot of money

Child of the past
Is dirty and grubby
Child of the present
Is sometimes muddy

Child of the past
Opens the cab door latch
Child of the present
Plays a game of hopscotch

Child of the past
Feels sick and weak
Child of the present
Plays hide-and-seek

Child of the past
Feels very sad
Child of the present
Is all happy and glad

Child of the past
Looks like he saw a ghost
Child of the present
Eats yummy toast.

Lisa McMahon (11)
St Mark's Primary School, Dunmurry

Child

Child of the past
Sleeping on the ground
Child of the present
Sleeps as snug as a hound

Child of the past
Has no games to play
Child of the present
Plays games and laughs all day

Child of the past
Is weak and bony
Child of the present
Is never lonely

Child of the past
Has nothing to eat
Child of the present
Can eat with his feet

Child of the past
Works in the dark
Child of the present
Goes to the park

Child of the past
Has clothes ragged and ripped
Child of the present
Has a jacket with a zip

Child of the past
Gets hit with a cane
Child of the present
Is told don't do it again.

Michael Lyons (11)
St Mark's Primary School, Dunmurry

Child

Child of the past
Lives in a very rowdy house
Child of the present
Lives in a house as silent as a mouse

Child of the past
Has nowhere to sleep not even a shattered old shed
Child of the present
Sleeps in a nice, comfortable bed

Child of the past
Has no nice games to play
Child of the present
Has a beautiful day

Child of the past
Goes to work instead of school
Child of the present
Goes to school and when he gets home
He goes to the pool

Child of the past
Has clothes ragged and ripped
Child of the present
Has a very warm coat
And a jacket that's zipped

Child of the past
Has no food to spare
Child of the present
Has food that he could share

Child of the past
Feels weak and sad
Child of the present
Feels very happy and glad.

James Todd (11)
St Mark's Primary School, Dunmurry

Child

Child of the past
No bed to sleep in
Not even a home
Child of the present
A bed full of teddies
Beside my brother Eddie's

Child of the past
Having no fun
Child of the present
Having a laugh
Lying out in the sun

Child of the past
Wearing old dirty clothes
Child of the present
Wearing new clean clothes

Child of the past
Selling all their wares
To get a penny or two
Child of the present
Don't need to sell
They have enough money
To buy two buses

Child of the past
Lucky to have an old rope
Child of the present
A room full of toys and lots of ice cream

Child of the past
Learning a bit at school
But can't concentrate at all
Child of the present
Lots of new things to learn
And study after role call

Child of the past
Sad and hungry
Nothing to be excited about
Child of the present
Happy and glad
Lots of things to look forward to.

Jennifer Kerr (11)
St Mark's Primary School, Dunmurry

Child

Child of the past
Cold on a stone

Child of the present
Snuggled up at home

Child of the past
Eats from a bin

Child of the present
Drinks Coke from a tin

Child of the past
Playing with marbles

Child of the present
Throwing some cobbles

Child of the past
Clothes covered in soot

Child of the present
Wearing a tracksuit

Child of the past
All weak and sad

Child of the present
Strong and glad.

Gerard McKeown (11)
St Mark's Primary School, Dunmurry

Child

Child of the past
Having an uncomfortable night
Child of the present
Snuggled in bed so tight

Child of the past
Wearing rags and tight hats
Child of the present
Wearing warm scarves and combats

Child of the past
Working in cold, damp mills
Child of the present
Playing happily on the hills

Child of the past
Can neither read nor write
Child of the present
Intelligent and bright

Child of the past
Weak, tired and sad
Child of the present
Smiling happily, joyful and glad

Child of the past
Wandering about the cold, damp alleys
Child of the present
Having lots of fun in the warm, sunny valleys.

Bronagh McKenna (11)
St Mark's Primary School, Dunmurry

Child

Child of the past
Sleeping in a bed with
All of his brothers and sisters
Child of the present
Sleeping in a bed with
Only himself in it

Child of the past
With rags for clothes and
Only water and bread to eat
Child of the present
All beautiful clothes and
Vegetables and all sorts of meat

Child of the past
Goes out to sell all sorts of fruit
Child of the present
Goes to school every day and learns

Child of the past
Playing skipping and hopping games
Child of the present
Playing football or PC games

Child of the past
Feels very sad and unhappy
Child of the present
Feels very happy and cheerful.

Laura Allen (11)
St Mark's Primary School, Dunmurry

Child

Child of the past
Lives in streets and alleys
And sleeps on lumpy ground.
Child of the present
Lives in warm house and sleeps in a bed
With blankets wrapped around.

Child of the past
Ragged clothes and bare feet.
Child of the present
Nike and Air Max to comfort their feet.

Child of the past
Works long hard hours
Only some learn to read and write.
Child of the present
Goes to school for six hours
Then plays until night.

Child of the past
Girl plays with hoops and ropes
But still feels sad and weak.
Child of the present
Plays Game Boys and in parks
Feeling so happy at the end of the school week.

Ciara Moylan (10)
St Mark's Primary School, Dunmurry

The Great Manchester United Haiku

Man United won
At the disgraceful Anfield
Yesterday morning.

Kevin Quinn (10)
St Mark's Primary School, Dunmurry

Child

Child of the past
Sleeping in the streets
All cold and wet
Child of the present
Sleeping in a bed
All warm and dry

Child of the past
No money for food
Can only have a bit of bread
Child of the present
Money for food
Can eat what he wants

Child of the past
With rags for clothes
And no shoes on his feet
Child of the present
With brand new clothes
And shoes to wear

Child of the past
Working during the day with no rest
Child of the present
Goes to school to learn and gets a rest

Child of the past
Playing games like skipping and hopping
Child of the present
Playing board games and dance mats

Child of the past
Feeling tired and lonely with no place to go
Child of the present
Feeling happy and glad to be safe.

Kelly McCleave (11)
St Mark's Primary School, Dunmurry

Days, Days And Other Days

The rain falls,
It bounces off the walls,
It splashes off the ground,
it flows through the town.

It shines at my feet,
It lights up the dark street.

Every day's a grey day,
Every day's a play day.

Then there are those cloudy days,
When the sky goes all different ways.

Blue days,
Always have their ways,
Like when you're feeling down,
When everything seems dark and brown.

Nothing days are when you just want to sit and watch TV,
Just to sit on someone's knee.

Siobhán McCullough (9)
St Mark's Primary School, Dunmurry

My Family

My family are gentle people who think of me when I am down,
If I were a judge I would give my mum or dad a golden crown,
My sister is so lonely so I play with her a lot,
But when I fall out with her my brother says, 'Drat!'
My brother is so selfish, but then most brothers are,
I think I like him so I'll think of him like a star.

Angela Diamond (10)
St Mark's Primary School, Dunmurry

Rules

Do not pounce on wrinkled grandmas,
Do not waken sleeping mas,
Don't wear dungarees to dinner,
Do not try to reach the stars.

Do not smile at hungry tigers,
Do not leap on top of dogs,
Do not laugh at pudgy pandas,
Do not try to wrestle frogs.

Do not walk in what a cat's done,
Do not dance around for hours,
Don't be cheeky to your teacher,
They have too much power.

Do not ask a shark to babysit
Your baby brother in his cot,
And whatever else you do
It is better you . . .
Do not!

Lisa McAreavey (9)
St Mark's Primary School, Dunmurry

Colours

If I were blue I'd be the sea
Glistening in the sun.

If I were green
I'd be a grassy spear
Blowing in the wind.

If I were red
I'd be a sunbathing rose.

If I were yellow
I'd be sunbeams
Keeping the Earth warm.

Taylor Murtagh (8)
St Mark's Primary School, Dunmurry

Rules

Do not jump in rushing water
Do not bite a blackbird's butt
Do not dance with smelly daughters
Do not pick at slimy cuts.

Do not bounce on rusty bed springs
Do not lie in a cold bath
Do not wear slippers in a sauna
Never make hyenas laugh.

Jackie Johnson (9)
St Mark's Primary School, Dunmurry

Christmas Eve

Christmas Eve and magic's growing
The robin's red breast is proudly showing
My wish for all, is peace on Earth,
Let's celebrate the baby's birth.

It happens once every year
In this place, it happens here
Waiting for the day to come
While the children have a bit of fun.

Samantha Murphy (10)
St Mark's Primary School, Dunmurry

Rules

Do not spring on hidden tigers
Do not stand near sewer rats
Do not awaken flaming fire fiends
Do not wear exploding hats.
Never go near crackling dragons
Do not follow shooting stars
Do not steal an ape's bananas
Do not eat a lunch of flowers.

Ryan Magee (9)
St Mark's Primary School, Dunmurry

My Precious Family

My family are very caring, sharing and sometimes very bossy,
They are funny, kind and they are also very loving
I don't know what I would do without them
They have always been there for me when I am down,
My sister is fun to share secrets with.
My brothers fight a lot but I love them just the way they are.

My mummy and daddy love me so much
They call me all sorts of things, like 'my little princess' and 'angel'
I never feel lonely in my house, it's sort of like the never-ending story.

Shauna Hamill (10)
St Mark's Primary School, Dunmurry

Football Fanatics

Sheffield's stadium sparkled splendidly on Sheffield's stands.
Manchester's mascots made mad noise in Man Utd's match
Liverpool's lights landed lightly on Liverpool's left back.
Celtic's crowd clapped for Celtic's centre midfielder.
Sunderland's stands stood silently in Sunderland's stands.
Plymouth's players played powerfully on Plymouth's pitch.
Arsenal and Aston Villa arranged a match at Anfield.

Arsenal went ahead.

Marcus Owens (10)
St Mark's Primary School, Dunmurry

Footie Skills

Six sneaky Southampton supporters stole shorts, socks and shirts.
Celtic's chief cried, 'Chase the centre forward!'
Fulham's fierce full forward fired five shots in the far post.
Portsmouth prepared to perform penalties in the Premiership.
Liverpool's Le-Tallec launched lightly a lovely shot.
Chelsea's Crespo chipped Charlton's courageous, cunning keeper.

Daragh McGuinness (10)
St Mark's Primary School, Dunmurry

Mixed Up Christopher

My ears are made of red books
My arms are made of blue skies
My legs are made of solid gold
My feet are made of mince pies.

My head is made of silly babies
My hair is made of little soldiers
My knees are made of apple pie
My nose is made of big boulders.

My thoughts are made of star names
My dreams are made of light nights
My wishes are made of light love
My feelings are made of dark nights.

I'm all mixed up as you can see
And all that's here I'm glad to be.

Christopher Herald (9)
St Mark's Primary School, Dunmurry

My Heart Is Made Of Fire

My heart is made of flaming fire
My arms are made of buzzing bees
My mouth is made of concrete carpet
My eyes are made of big blue seas.

My nose is made of holey cheese
My ears are made of mushy peas
My chin is made of a prickly pin
So why am I like tin?

My dreams are made of nice things
My thoughts are made of dopey dogs
My feelings are like itchy fleas
So I wish someone would be like me.

Aidan Devlin (9)
St Mark's Primary School, Dunmurry

My Family

I have a family
Who are very good to me
They are kind and gentle

When I'm lonely
They comfort me
They show respect
To others

You could tell them
Anything
You wouldn't feel ashamed
We could laugh until midnight
And then go to bed and cuddle up

I have a special family
Because I have an angel
That can guide me.

Niamh Walker (10)
St Mark's Primary School, Dunmurry

Matt's Cat

Matt's cat was too fat,
so he put her on a diet.
For days and days
he fed her hay
until she nearly faded away.

So he gave her fish
and steak and meat
until she couldn't
see her feet.

Matt's cat was too fat,
but he liked her
just like that.

Matthew O'Donnell (10)
St Mark's Primary School, Dunmurry

One Original Owl

One original owl overtook an octopus.
Two thoughtless tramps teased the tender tigers.
Three tough teachers taste the tropical tea.
Four fierce footballers fought for the football.
Five frightened farmers fled from the fireworks.
Six sensitive skunks smelled the sunflowers.
Seven silly servants stole a slippery seal.
Eight evil emperors explored England.
Nine nervous newts were numb for nine minutes.
Ten tropical fish teased the Titanic.

James Norney (10)
St Mark's Primary School, Dunmurry

The World

The world is a lovely place,
I've never been to space.

I live in Ireland,
But I'd like to live on Hawaii Island.

But I'll never leave my friends,
So let's give this poem an end.

Naomi Smith (9)
St Mark's Primary School, Dunmurry

A School Poem

Two tall tame teachers tilted to teach class two
The delicious, drippy dinners did dances with desserts
Weary work always goes on forever
The respecting rules, ruled the school
The patient pupils picked on primary fours
The blind bats bit and battered the big books.

Maria Adams (10)
St Mark's Primary School, Dunmurry

Child

Child of the past
Sleeping on ground on a front door step
Child of the present
Sleeping in a very warm bed

Child of the past
Eating scraps off the ground and bins
Child of the present
Eating nice hot dinners with a happy grin

Child of the past
Having ripped rags for clothes to wear
Child of the present
Has a full selection of clothes and footwear

Child of the past
Playing dominoes and marbles by the train station
Child of the present
Playing Sims and Here Comes The Pain on PlayStations

Child of the past
Only learning the slightest bit of work
Child of the present
Learning lots of things to gain knowledge

Child of the past
Playing skipping and hoops
Child of the present
Playing football and boxing

Child of the past
Sad, weary and uncomfortable sitting by a bin
Child of the present
Happy and comfortable with the place he is in.

Dean McDonagh (11)
St Mark's Primary School, Dunmurry

Child

Child of the past
Lying in a doorway
Child of the present
Has a nice place to sleep

Child of the past
No food to spare
Child of the present
Has food for teddy bear

Child of the past
Having no fun
Child of the present
Having a ball in the sun

Child of the past
Working for little pay
Child of the present
At school learning most of the day

Child of the past
Opening the cab door
Child of the present
Dancing about the floor

Child of the past
All cold and damp
Child of the present
All warm, ready to turn off the lamp

Child of the past
Tired, upset, hurt, cold, unhappy and sad
Child of the present
Joyful, happy, warm and glad.

Rachel Whelan (11)
St Mark's Primary School, Dunmurry

Child

Child of the past
Sleeping on the street,
So cold, child nearly dead
Child of the present
All snug and warm in bed,
With a soft, fluffy pillow under his head

Child of the past
Selling for hours, getting no money,
Roaming the cold and chilly streets
Child of the present
All gay and happy,
Eating a sweet with shoes on his feet

Child of the past
Sitting in the streets, so lonely and dark
Child of the present
Playing with his friends happily in the park

Child of the past
Hardly any clothes at all
Child of the present
Has lots and lots
And he and Paul are having a ball

Child of the past
Working hard in a factory at light
Child of the present
Oh what a sight, he's only seven
And he can read and write.

Caoimhe McDonald (11)
St Mark's Primary School, Dunmurry

Child

Child of the past
All dirty and ragged
Child of the present
All clean and sharp

Child of the past
Nothing much to eat
Child of the present
Lots of vegetables and meat

Child of the past
No games, no fun
Child of the present
Very happy to be young

Child of the past
No home and alone
Child of the present
Lots of friends and a home

Child of the past
Working hard all day
Child of the present
All fun, all play

Child of the past
Sad, hurt and no one to care
Child of the present
Happy, joyful and cared for.

Amanda O'Prey (11)
St Mark's Primary School, Dunmurry

Child

Child of the past
Sleeping behind a cold stone
Child of the present
Sleeping in a warm home

Child of the past
Wearing old ragged clothes
Child of the present
Wearing new clean clothes

Child of the past
Having no fun at all
Child of the present
Playing with his new red ball

Child of the past
So cold and lonely
Child of the present
So warm and cosy

Child of the past
Finding food on the ground
Child of the present
Buying food out of town

Child of the past
Feeling scared and sad
Child of the present
Feeling happy and glad.

Jonathan Donnelly (11)
St Mark's Primary School, Dunmurry

Friend

Friends are nice and have good advice,
Friends are fun and bring the sun.
Friends are shy but can make you fly,
Friends are funny and some love bunnies.

Friends never let you down.

Samantha Gourley (10)
St Mark's Primary School, Dunmurry

Space

People wonder what's up there
In vast space.
They wonder if aliens exist.
The answer is this.

Up there are planets,
Stars and distant suns,
Asteroids, satellites, comets,
Galaxies and anti matter.

The scientists study
The sky with giant
Telescopes and look
For aliens with satellite dishes.

That's what's up there.

Andrew Gunn (10)
St Michael's Primary School, Belfast

Winter

It is winter, it is cold
And I am being very bold
Throwing snowballs in the air
And without any care
I hit an old man and he
Fell to the ground
And the snow fell on him in a mound
I went to my mum and dad
Being very sad
I told them what I'd done
And they said I was a very bad son.

Matthew McCormick (11)
St Michael's Primary School, Belfast

Sometimes I Wish

Sometimes I wish I didn't have to be me
I could be someone entirely different
But then again, I'd miss everyone
Sometimes I wish.

Sometimes I wish for something exciting
Even something a little crazy
But I'd miss my life
Sometimes I wish.

Sometimes I wish for something amazing
Something out of the ordinary
But then I wouldn't be me
Sometimes I wish.

Sometimes, just sometimes, I wish.

Laura Vinelott (11)
St Michael's Primary School, Belfast

School

One day I went to school,
But little did I know I was such a fool.
The teacher was mad,
And the work was really bad.
We kicked him out the door,
And we were bored no more!

Alice Donaldson (11)
St Michael's Primary School, Belfast

The Jungle

In the jungle,
There was such a rumble,
Between the monkey and the trees.
The monkey said the tree gave him fleas.
And the tree said the monkey kept on ruining his leaves.

Odhran McIntaggart (11)
St Michael's Primary School, Belfast

Double Chemistry Session

Chemicals gushing
People rushing
Oh no don't let that smash!
We hear a terrible crash

We hear a slow rasp
Out of my mouth emits a gasp
I saw the mess on the floor
Right! Out the door!

Comes the sound of the school bell
Urgh! What's that smell?
I hear an explosion, a blow
Oh no, oh no, oh no!

Get out of here now!
But how? How . . . ?
Now I'm staying here, at home
Because the school has blown!

It might raise your hair
But you see I was there
Never will I go to a science lesson
Especially not a *double chemistry session!*

Eithne Fraser (11)
St Michael's Primary School, Belfast

Today

Today on my way to school
I fell into a pool
I nearly drowned
But found a pound
And now I'm called Mr Fool.

Timothy Durkan (10)
St Michael's Primary School, Belfast

School

On Wednesday I went to school,
If I didn't I would be such a fool.
On the way I saw a bull.
I went into school and sat on a stool.
I looked up at the notice board,
Oh look, there is a new rule.

James Day (11)
St Michael's Primary School, Belfast

Jim

I once met a boy called Jim,
There's no one quite like him!
He's perfect in every way,
There's nothing more to say!
In my heart he'd never fail,
If only he was real!

Emma Nicholson (10)
St Michael's Primary School, Belfast

Which Hobbies?

My favourite hobby is sport,
But then there's building a fort.
I don't know what I like.
I quite like cycling my bike.
Honestly I don't know
That's it! I like playing the *piano!*

Leenane Mellotte (10)
St Michael's Primary School, Belfast

My Cat

My cat is very fluffy,
She is very puffy,
Because she has eaten
All the seating.

My cat is black and white
Her eyesight isn't very good,
Because she banged into the light,
Then she was in a bad mood.

The dog across the road barked,
My cat ran away,
Her fur is now marked,
With the scar she got on that day.

Siofra Berndt (10)
St Michael's Primary School, Belfast

Shorty

With his big flabby cheeks
Where he stores his meal
In the middle of the night
When he runs on his wheel
I just have to call
And he will come
To me in his ball
He is so cute and furry
He likes to bury
His sunflower seeds
His little black eyes
Look like two beads
He is my pet hamster, Shorty.

Ryan McGuckin (11)
St Michael's Primary School, Belfast

My Rabbit Junior

Junior is
What Junior does,
And Junior eats
What Junior wants,
And Junior stays
Awake at night,
And dreams about
The morning.

Junior is brown,
With floppy ears,
She's big, she's bold,
She never fears,
And Junior's sister, Norbert,
Who's as white as can be,
Has pink eyes,
An albino bunny!

But Junior ran
Away last year,
And of her now,
I'll never hear.
But even though
We're far apart
Junior still lies
Upon my heart.

Isobel Clarke (10)
St Michael's Primary School, Belfast

Jackie Chan

Jackie Chan is a great stuntman,
If he can't do it no one can,
Jackie Chan acts in Rush Hour 2,
Along with his sidekick, Chris Tucker, too,
Jackie Chan can fight like hell,
If you got one of his kicks you could tell!

Declan King (11)
St Michael's Primary School, Belfast

My Pet

My mum bought a dog
It went to the toilet on a log.
My daddy told him off
So he began to cough.
My dog got sick
So I took him to the vet quick.

When we took him home again
He was just the same old pain.
He bit my shoes
And did big poos.
He ate all my food
Bet it was tasty and good.

Every time I was asleep
He came out to take a peep.
Every morning he took a bath
He would run down the path.
Even though he is the same old pain
He's my dog all over again.

Erin Sykes (11)
St Michael's Primary School, Belfast

The Boat Note

There was a girl,
Who had hair that curled,
That travelled the world,
And in her boat,
She wrote a note
And then she sent it afloat,
When she threw it into the sea,
Guess who found it, me,
I looked at the writing,
It was very frightening,
And that was the end of me.

Roisin McAlister (11)
St Michael's Primary School, Belfast

The Ghostly Cooker

A ghost is living in my room,
It haunts me day and night,
Hiding in the darkness and gloom,
It's ready to give me a fright.

I can hear its desperate wailing,
And smell its smoky smell,
Through the air I think it's sailing,
With ghosts you just can't tell!

Transparent is the ghost,
Which haunts me day by day,
It needs to join its host,
But cannot find its way.

I get an eerie feeling,
Whenever it is near,
I look up at my ceiling,
Then sigh and think, *oh dear!*

The ghost is like a stormy cloud,
That follows me around,
Its wailing seems to be getting loud,
And coming from the ground.

Mum thinks it's just the cooker,
In the kitchen under my room,
But we know it's a secret looker,
Trying to send me to my doom!

Eve Kells (11)
St Michael's Primary School, Belfast

School

Today I was such a fool,
I fell into a pool,
I heard a big sound,
Found a hundred pound,
And never went back to school.

Rebekah McCann (10)
St Michael's Primary School, Belfast

Snow

I don't want rain! No! No!
I want lots of snow.
Weather forecast just shows rain.
We want snow in Ireland again.

Snow is cold,
That's what I've been told.
I wouldn't know
Because we never have snow!

Hi ho! Hi ho! Here comes the snow!
We'll laugh all day,
And play, play, play!
Hi ho! Hi ho! Here comes the snow!

Michael McGarry (11)
St Michael's Primary School, Belfast

Hate

Hate is black like the formless void.
It tastes like cold death.
It smells rotten and deceased.
It looks like the fear of others.
It sounds like life ending.
It feels like guilt of actions done in the past.

Conal Mulholland (11)
St Michael's Primary School, Belfast

Family And Friends

My friend is big, as big as me,
My mum is small as a pea,
My dad is chubby as a big fat doughnut,
And I am normal, as normal as can be.

Damien Dornan (10)
St Michael's Primary School, Belfast

The World Is Being Destroyed

The world is beautiful,
all the nature,
all the old sights.

The world is beautiful,
with all the oceans,
and all the rivers.

The world is beautiful,
with the sky,
and with the birds.

The world is beautiful,
with all the trees,
and all the flowers.

The world is beautiful,
but we destroy it.
We cover it with pollution,
we cut down the trees,
we just build and build,
we just can't go on.
But we just can't stop.

Jacob Agee (11)
St Michael's Primary School, Belfast

Christina

Christina is my favourite pop star
I don't think she'd make a good rock star
She had blonde hair and now it's black.
She's got big blue eyes
And is very wise
I don't care what they say, she's going to make it anyway
That's alright, that's OK, she doesn't care what you say!

Kieva Rainey (10)
St Michael's Primary School, Belfast

Fighting Friends

'Where is Laura?' said Mum watching telly one day
'If you're bored why don't you ask her round to play?'
'I can't,' I said, 'we've fallen out,
On the way home from school she started to shout.

Coming out the door, I tugged her hair,
I didn't mean to, it's so unfair.
I could have done it harder if I wanted to,
But she ran off crying and said, 'I hate you!'
She's a cry baby if you ask me.
No way is she coming round for tea.

I'm not saying sorry,
I don't care what you say,
And Laura is not coming round to play!'

Cassie Moane (11)
St Michael's Primary School, Belfast

A Witch

A witch is selfish, ugly and cruel,
She's dumb and plump
So she'll never get a date.
She hides away in the forests
Learning how to fly and cast her spells
To make it rain, shine and storm.
A witch's face is warty, a witch's hair is split
A witch's eyes are baggy, so she's ugly on every bit.
A witch's clothes are weird
The colours are black, white and purple
The clothes are stained and ripped
And that's what makes a witch selfish, ugly and cruel.

Catherine Crawford (10)
St Michael's Primary School, Belfast

Silence

Silence is a lovely thing
It's soft and comforting
You can hear the heartbeat
In the silence of your street.

Silence is so peaceful
And it's very safe
Sometimes I feel scared
In a room all alone.

Silence gives you time to think
When I am in silence I can
Be in a wee world of my own.

Silence is so calm
Remembering all the memories
I have had is silence.

Anna Lyttle (10)
St Michael's Primary School, Belfast

Who Would I Like To Be?

Who would I like to be
When I am 30, when I am 3.
Would I like to be someone
Splashing near the sea?
What about someone
Stuck up an apple tree,
Climbing up, climbing down,
Seeing stuff you have never seen.
Or what about an explorer, meeting people
And going places you have never been!
But wait; who would I like to be . . .
Young, beautiful just like me.

Rebecca Hollywood (10)
St Michael's Primary School, Belfast

Cinderella

In the dead of night, jewels and all,
The ugly sisters set off to the ball,
While Cinderella, in the dirty cellar,
Was left behind to clean.
She swept, she dusted, she flubberbusted,
Until she could take no more.
With a scream and a fight
She yelled, 'Tonight, fairy, please come and take me away,'
In a flash of light, and the crash of a car
The fairy was there by her side.

'I want a pink rose, and silver pantyhose
With a bright blue dress
And light brown shoes, two of those.'
'Hold on, hold on!' yelled the fairy,
'One at a time.'
With a click, and a swick
That's just what she got.

She went to the ball, but that is not all
She hated the food, and the prince was so rude
She left in a huff
And said, 'That's enough.
Next time I'll be wary of calling that fairy.
I'll just stay at home.
And be on my own.'

Sarah Louise Carey (10)
St Michael's Primary School, Belfast

Chaos

Pretty Miss Pruffet
Sat on a tuffet
Eating her bread and jam.
A spider came down
Wearing shoes and a gown
And said to her,
'I prefer ham!'

Jill and Jack
Were coming back
From Old McDonald's zoo.
The lions had been saying, 'Oink!'
And the monkeys were saying, 'Moo!'

A silly pig had gone
To a market in town that day.
He went to buy his things
And found he had no money to pay.

A crooked man and his crooked cat
Had found a crooked house.
But when they entered the house
They found a crooked mouse.

Old Jack Sprat's wife
Was reading magazines
While Sprat himself
Was eating chips and beans.

Catherine O'Neill (10)
St Michael's Primary School, Belfast

My Little Brother

My little brother called Tom
Can be cute at times.
Don't get me wrong
If he gets bullied,
Boy, I'll be worried
About my cute lil' brother called Tom.

When I'm at home in a bad mood
He comes over and gets me worked up
With his homework, his PlayStation and his stink bombs
That's my annoying lil' brother called Tom.

If I hurt him a small bit,
He'll kick and hurt me back
Just last week I found out
He'd gone and cracked my back,
With one of his heavy stink bombs
That's my terrible bro' called Tom.

Caroline McCusker (10)
St Michael's Primary School, Belfast

Autumn

Autumn, autumn,
Autumn's here
All the mist, the rain and snow
It's back, it's back again

It's cold, it's warm
I don't know
All I want is snow, snow, snow!

Let's make a snowman
Let's call him Dan
What about that now? That's a plan!

Now it's over
Let's go in, can't wait to tomorrow
To come out again!

Naomi Rose Flynn (10)
St Michael's Primary School, Belfast

If I Had A Wish

If I had a wish
I would maybe be a millionaire
I would be so happy
Water beds! Jacuzzis and
things of that sort!

If I had a wish
I would maybe quit school
I would be so happy
No work! Stay up late and
things of that sort!

If I had a wish
I would maybe travel the world
I would be so happy
Beaches! Sunshine and
things of that sort!

If I had a wish!

Aoife Jackson (11)
St Michael's Primary School, Belfast

I Wish I Had A Dog!

I wish I had a dog,
A big friendly one,
With black fur all over,
It would be my best friend.

I would play with it every day,
All kinds of games like fetch,
I would call it Ross,
And say, 'You're the boss!'

I wish I had a dog,
A big sporty one,
With black fur all over,
It would be my best friend.

Peter Leggett (11)
St Michael's Primary School, Belfast

The Place Under My Bed

There is a place under my bed,
It really is quite creepy,
If I lose something I always find it under there
Because I kick it in when I'm sleepy.

My mum keeps asking me to tidy it,
But I really can't be bothered.
It's like a jungle under there,
I never could get under.

When I look under from what I can see
It's like another planet far away from me.
It smells quite bad from smelly socks,
I wouldn't be surprised if I found a fox.

I borrowed a pair of shoes from my sister,
I hope she didn't want them back!
Anyway I'm sure before they got in
They were already black!

Yesterday I got in trouble in school,
'Where's your jotter?' my teacher said
'Oh no!' my reply was . . .
'In the jungle under my bed!'

Rachel McCann (10)
St Michael's Primary School, Belfast

The Fat Mouse

There was a fat mouse,
That didn't have a house,
I found it sitting around in my garden.

I picked it up,
And brought it inside
But then my mum told me
That it was a stone.

Ciaran Kelly (11)
St Michael's Primary School, Belfast

My Cats

Molly and Polly are my cats
When they get dirty
They look like two black rats

But they don't seem to care.

They think they're the boss
They think they will get what they want.
We know they won't.

But they don't seem to care.

And then there's clawing the furniture,
And urinating beside the litter tray,
We say it's got to stop,

But they don't seem to care.

But, hey, when they're asleep,
They're cute lying on the bed,
Snug on the bed covers they purr.

But we don't seem to care, do we?

Nathalie McGrillen (10)
St Michael's Primary School, Belfast

Heaven Eyes

Heaven Eyes is so sacred,
Cobwebs, draw through her fingers,
Her eyes, light blue and shiny.
Still as can be, they linger.
Her body is so fragile-looking and so pale.
Heaven Eyes is a girl
Who watches, waiting in wonder.

Maedbh Donaghy (10)
St Michael's Primary School, Belfast

Lucky Irish

There once was an Irish man who
Always fought a Spanish man.
The Spanish man used guns while
The Irish man used a leprechaun.
They fought all night, they fought all day
With a leprechaun from Galway Bay.

The Irish man always seemed to win,
When he fought over the Shannon.
From Antrim to Kerry,
To the fields of Derry.
But when in Spain
It always seemed to rain
Therefore it was postponed.
In the end the Irish man won the cup,
While the Spanish man was thrown in muck.

James Mulligan (11)
St Michael's Primary School, Belfast

My Goldfish Fishy

My goldfish Fishy lives in a bowl in a kitchen in a house
This goldfish of mine is the size of a small brown mouse.
It feels so slippery, slimy and scaly.
Every day it has its daily glare out of the bowl and into the air.
I got it in a pet shop over in the corner.
There was another boy, his second name was Horner.
My goldfish Fishy likes his meal
Every Friday like the deal.
He doesn't like being handled
Or too much food in his bowl.
But my goldfish Fishy is my biggest goal.

Michael Guirov (10)
St Michael's Primary School, Belfast